ENOUGH ROOM FOR JOY

ENOUGH ROOM FOR JOY

The Early Days of Jean Vanier's L'Arche

Bill Clarke

BlueBridge

Cover design by Angel Guerra

*Cover image (insert): L'Arche Trosly—the original home where it all began
(photo courtesy of Kevin Burns)*

Layout by Christiane Lemire

Library of Congress Cataloging-in-Publication Data

Clarke, Bill.
Enough room for joy : the early days of Jean Vanier's l'Arche / Bill Clarke.
      p. cm.
ISBN-13: 978-1-933346-06-9
ISBN-10: 1-933346-06-X
1. Arche (Association)—History. 2. Church work with people with mental disabilities.
3. Vanier, Jean, 1928- I. Title.

BX2347.8.M4C53 2007
267'.182—dc22   2006035272

Published in the United States of America in 2007 by
B l u e B r i d g e
An imprint of
United Tribes Media Inc.
240 West 35th Street, Suite 500
New York, NY 10001

www.bluebridgebooks.com

Printed in the United States of America

10 9 8 7 6 5 4 3 2 1

Contents

To all my brothers and sisters in l'Arche,
including the many who have passed through the veil
into the fullness of community.

Foreword

I have just finished reading Bill's book and my heart is filled with thanksgiving. Sometimes my memory fails before the pressures of the present. It is good to relive what God has done in His Arche. For it is true, this is His work and not ours.

There is yet much opaqueness in our communities, as in myself, as in each of us. Many things that prevent the Spirit living freely. But I know that Jesus came to heal and to pardon. Also, there have been many deep failures. I think with sadness of the seven men and women we put back into the psychiatric hospital in spite of promises made to them. God knows our weaknesses.

Bill has accentuated the joys and the sufferings and our fragility, but he has rarely spoken of our real weaknesses and infidelities. It is true that it is not easy for him to do so, not because these are not evident, but because of his reverence for others. We have yet a lot to learn, and even more, we must deepen daily our love and our professional skills.

Yes, I am thankful for the past, I rejoice in the present and I await the future with expectancy and confidence.

I trust that as we evolve – and God knows things are changing so fast at l'Arche and the Arches throughout the world – we will remain faithful to our call: live day by day in mutual love and acceptance, dependent upon the Spirit striving to form one community, open to new expansion and to welcoming the most wounded, growing in competency to help all to grow.

Will you pray for that? Pray that as we become known through this book and others that we will keep that initial simplicity and poverty and a desire to be present to wounded people, to help them evolve and to evolve with them.

Please, do not feel that you must come to l'Arche to visit us – do not think that we are something special. There is a real danger today of our being overcome by visitors – good-willed and eager to help or to imitate us. Rather, in the silence of your heart join us in communion with the Spirit of God who is Love, Compassion, and Truth. Commit yourselves to the wounded ones near you today. Listen to them, seek to be with them, grow with them in mutual respect and love. Then all of us can join hands spiritually and seek each in his or her own way to make our world a place of peace, of universal love and brotherhood where God is the Father of all, however handicapped or intelligent they may be.

As my life calls me to assume new responsibilities, and to travel from country to country, I am acutely aware that others are *living* what I am but *preaching*. To talk, I know, is important. It is good that the message be known. But it is more important to live and to live fully as my brothers and sisters of l'Arche are living – to live in obscurity without fame, only in love and tender compassion.

I thank Jesus for them, for Raphaël, for Guru and so many. I thank Him for this family of which I am a part – for they have given me life.

Jean Vanier
Asha Niketan
Calcutta, India, December 1973

Thirty-two years haved passed since I wrote the foreword to Bill's book *Enough Room for Joy*. As Bill says, since then l'Arche has grown and deepened and our world has changed. L'Arche remains its fragile self, with its weaknesses and its strengths. Our people are as beautiful as ever. It is such a privilege to be with them and together to be a sign of hope.

Jean Vanier
L'Arche, Trosly-Breuil, France, December 2005

Introduction

A couple of years ago while I was visiting with the communities of l'Arche in Australia, several people came forward asking me to autograph copies of *Enough Room for Joy*, a book I had written over 30 years ago. It pleased me that this book, which had been out of print for a number of years, was still being read with interest by people living on the other side of the world (and a very beautiful side it is). Over the years, many have told me how this book has touched them and helped them to discover the gift of l'Arche and its message of hope. Thus, when Kevin Burns of Novalis in Canada approached me about reissuing it, I was not taken totally by surprise, and sensed that, even though so much has changed in l'Arche and in our world, this book still has something to say to us today.

As I revisited the original text, a few things were immediately obvious to me. Clearly, the l'Arche of those early days was much less complex. Today it is an international federation of about 130 communities in 30 countries on five continents, with all that this implies of linguistic, cultural, and even religious diversity. Jean Vanier continues to have a spiritual influence on the community that he co-founded with Père Thomas, Philippe, and Raphaël, but l'Arche is now the responsibility of an international board, of which Jean is no longer a member. Nevertheless, in its essence l'Arche remains fundamentally the same unique and revolutionary community that has — or, rather, is — a message of profound significance for our times. The world itself has undergone tremendous changes in the past 35 years, changes that place it in even more dire need of the kind of hope offered by little communities such as l'Arche. They demonstrate that there is a way for the rich and the poor, the weak and the strong, and people of different languages, cultures, and religious beliefs to live together in creative harmony.

In September 2004 I had the privilege of spending some time with *Kana no ie* (Cana House), the l'Arche Community in Japan. There I experienced something of the same spirit of welcome and joy along with the pain and struggle that had so deeply touched me years ago on my first visit to the original l'Arche at Trosly-Breuil, in the north of France. At *Kana no ie* my pain and struggle involved trying several times each day to get and keep my stiff old legs crossed sufficiently to enable me to join the others sitting on the floor around the ankle-high dining table. Managing with chopsticks to convey rice and other delicacies from plate to mouth was a slightly less daunting challenge. But the smiles, the laughter, the gentle teasing all interspersed with moments of serious conversation and, on occasion, an angry outburst were reminiscent of l'Arche homes I have visited in France, Canada, India, Africa, Honduras, and elsewhere. It is from the life in these homes, at the heart of which are the people with developmental disabilities, that a common spirit emanates and endures through the years and across this ever-expanding international organization.

In the spring of 1980 I had gone to live and work at the Ignatius Farm Community in Guelph, Ontario. This community, although an enterprise of the Jesuits, owed its founding vision to l'Arche. Unlike l'Arche, it welcomed not only people with developmental disabilities, but also people coming out of the prison system, psychiatric care facilities, or other unhappy situations. Living in this community for over 20 years helped to keep me close to l'Arche and to deepen my appreciation for the beauty, the mystery, and the human impossibility of such communities. Only by the grace of God can they exist and survive. In June 2001, after much heartfelt searching, the Farm Community closed its doors; a very sad day for me and for many others. Over the years a few l'Arche communities have also gone under, and others are desperately struggling to stay afloat. The very precariousness of these communities is part of their grace and attraction. Would a rose be such a thing of beauty if it had the durability of a rock?

After the closing of the Farm Community I went to l'Arche in Trosly, for a sabbatical time of healing and rest. Stepping out of the car in which Barbara had driven me from Charles de Gaulle airport outside Paris, I was greeted by Paula, who tearfully informed me that Edith had just died. Edith had been one of the first residents welcomed into la Forestière, the home created 20 years earlier for people with more severe disabilities, and Paula had been living in that home with Edith for a number of years. Edith could not walk or talk or do very much of anything on her own. While she was very obese, she did have enough control over her left arm and hand to feed herself, with a little help from others. This left hand she also used to rain sudden and vicious blows on her own large head, the best way she knew to express her inner pain. Edith, one of nine siblings, at an early age had been given up by her overwrought mother and placed in an institution where she was confined, with little or no human interaction, until at the age of eighteen she was welcomed into l'Arche. Her large head was usually wrapped in bandages to soothe her self-inflicted wounds and to protect it from further abuse. There was, however, much life and sometimes fire in Edith's intense dark brown eyes. Out of those eyes radiated a powerful and sensitive personality.

During the prayer service following Edith's death, many talked about their relationship with her over the years. Chris spoke of how 20 years before, she had arrived at la Forestière from Quebec just in time to welcome Edith: "We were both teenagers at the time and we really have grown up together," Chris said. "She is the person who has most helped me to stay and to grow here in l'Arche." A monk, who two years earlier had taken six months away from his monastery to live at la Forestière, spoke of how Edith had shaped his priestly vocation. As the testimonies continued, it became more and more evident just what an extraordinary woman she was and how profoundly she had touched and transformed the lives of others. Edith's body, clothed in a white gown, was laid out in the little chapel of la Forestière. She looked incredibly peaceful and majestic, her whole body seeming to glow with an aura of light. I have never before or since seen a body look so beautiful. It was as if her spirit, now liberated into the fullness of life, was somehow still communing with the body that had been both burden and blessing throughout her painful earthly sojourn. A few days after the funeral, while we were walking towards la Forestière, Paula said to me, "You know, I can somehow understand God creating this magnificent universe with its galaxies of stars and all the wondrous things here on this earth, but what is totally beyond me is that God could create something as extraordinary as an Edith."

This story points to a significant change that has taken place at l'Arche since the early days. The community of Trosly and many others began to welcome people with more severe and multiple disabilities. People like Edith have been helping to highlight and to deepen what is the very essence of l'Arche. Since Edith could do so very little on her own, she revealed even more clearly the primacy of *being* over *doing*. She also invited those around her to a more contemplative presence, without which it would have been impossible to hear her inner cry and to access her inner beauty and gifts. The tenderness and sensitivity of a man like André, whose disability is much less severe, was always called forth on his regular visits to Edith's home. It was wonderful to see the gentleness that this usually wild and boisterous young man was capable of demonstrating toward Edith and her similarly challenged housemates. More important than the extensive expansion of l'Arche has been the deepening of its fundamental vision that each human person, however limited he or she may seem to be, is a sacred gift, a gift to be cherished and shared. It is becoming increasingly evident that people with disabilities are not only the heart of the communities, but are also their source of strength and unity.

This new edition of *Enough Room for Joy* has undergone only minor editorial changes. It speaks of l'Arche as it was at the beginning, especially at Trosly, and from this point of view it is, I believe, an important historical document. At the same time, it reveals the essential and unchanging gift of l'Arche.

One obvious and necessary correction to the original text is in how the people at the heart of the communities, the "core members," are identified. Thirty years ago, we were using the language of the times, which spoke of the "mentally handicapped." Fortunately, we now recognize the disrespect implicit in this way of speaking. Today we readily acknowledge that people ought not to be defined by their limitations or their gifts. They are, first and foremost, people – albeit people who have a learning or intellectual disability or a developmental disability. Different cultures tend to prefer one of these terms over another. I have chosen to use the latter term, "people with a developmental disability," which seems to be the phrase used most often in North America.

Thirty-five years ago I viewed l'Arche with a certain starry-eyed idealism. My long friendship with it, including six years as the pastoral minister to the International Council of l'Arche, has given me a more realistic view that includes the harsh reality of its many shortcomings and failings. I could write pages, even chapters, about the shadow side of l'Arche, but I have chosen to simply present the ideal as I saw it then. I know from personal experience that the leadership in l'Arche is very aware of the gap between the ideal and the lived reality in the various communities. In order to realistically face and deal with this gap, l'Arche embarked on a three-year federation-wide discernment process (now in its final stage) to claim as an entire body its mission and identity today. Rather than being disillusioned through these 35 years, I have gained an even deeper appreciation for the enduring validity of the vision and for the faith, courage, and wisdom that are being lived out in the humble daily circumstances of the various communities around the globe.

More than ever before, the human family, at risk of drowning in an ocean of division and violence, desperately needs signs of hope. I feel a sense of urgency to again present this exposition of one such sign, this fragile little Ark still boldly sailing on our world's stormy waters.

Several people mentioned in the book – Madame Vanier, Père Thomas, Raphaël, and others – have since passed on to their heavenly home. My memories of them, as well as the love and friendship of many sisters and brothers living today throughout the federation of l'Arche, are a continual source of life and inspiration to me. Thus it is to all of them that I dedicate this new edition. The first edition was dedicated to my own dear mother. Since she is now enjoying the company of Mammy Vanier, Raphaël, and the others, I'm sure she doesn't mind relinquishing her place on the dedication page.

1

Getting into the Ark

~

This book is about a new type of community that is rapidly spreading to different parts of the world, and that in a quiet way is calling to liberation people caught in, or victims of, a world of excessive individualism and competition.

L'Arche began in France in 1964 to give a permanent home to people with developmental disabilities. It seeks to unite these women and men and those who assist them into a single community, inspired by a spirit of loving acceptance that will help all its members develop to their fullest potential as human beings.

The word *l'Arche* is French for "the Ark." In the Bible story, Noah gathered the whole motley range of God's creatures into the Ark to save them from the great flood. So the Ark is symbolic of a place of refuge, of a community of great variety, and of the gift of hope.

My first contact with this community was through its founder, Jean Vanier. This happened in Montreal in the winter of 1964, at a national conference for university students engaged in the study of theology. The essence of Vanier's conferences was to communicate that the church and society not only have a mission to minister to the poor, but they very much *need* the poor. He spoke of how a certain group of "poor," people with developmental disabilities, has much to give to others in a variety of ways. If the church and society do not embrace these and other rejected people, church and society cannot be whole. He spoke of the need for communities that can bridge the gap between "rich" and "poor" of all kinds, and thus work towards uniting a divided world. Along with everyone else present, I was deeply touched by the simplicity and power of Vanier's message that clearly flowed from the depths of his own heart. Here was a man with a profound love for people, especially the most downtrodden – a man with a thirst for peace and unity. He was evidently drawing much inspiration from the people with whom he had chosen to share his life.

Thus it was that, when I went to Europe two years later, I arranged to spend a month at l'Arche. How vividly I can recall that trip, beginning from the turmoil of the dingy Gare du Nord train station in Paris. The one-hour train ride north toward Trosly-Breuil took me through squalid suburbs and then through gentle farmland and charming villages clustered around magnificent little fifteenth- and sixteenth-century churches – scenes I had admired in the paintings of the French Impressionists. Leaving the train at Compiègne, I again found myself in a city, but a city of 40,000, with nothing of the hustle and tumult of *gai Paris*. Someone was there to meet me and thus I was spared from waiting for the bus or trying to phone from the corner café to the constantly busy single telephone line at l'Arche. (They have since installed a switchboard, which has improved the situation only slightly.) The warmth and joyful spirit of the woman who greeted me put me immediately at ease. Barbara's disheveled appearance made it evident that clothes were one of her least concerns. She was obviously American, but her manner of driving indicated that she had lived in France long enough to acquire the reckless abandon and aggression that typifies the French way of handling a car – like a toy or a lethal weapon. After fifteen breathless minutes of driving, during which she chatted and laughed like an old friend and I tried not to appear too stunned, we turned off the highway into the peaceful little village of Trosly, population 900, nestled snugly against the beautiful Compiègne forest that rises around it on three sides. I noticed nothing special about this village – the community of l'Arche there simply occupies a scattered number of the old stone village houses – but I soon found myself absorbed in what seemed like a completely other world.

During this monthlong visit I spent my days in the workshop that does assembly work for a nearby plastics factory. It was not very complicated or challenging (just fit the red piece to the white piece and twist). But being there daily, side by side with Raphaël, Lucien, Jean-Luc, Norbert, and the others, sharing in their lives, their frustrations and occasional crises, their love for music and laughter, their joy, their concern for others, their faith – all this was to make me more deeply aware of the truth of the words I had heard from the lips of Jean Vanier many months earlier. I was "hooked."

The following summer I found the time to join a group from l'Arche on its annual pilgrimage. This one was to Fatima in Portugal. Here, again, it was the simplicity of these individuals that impressed me most. It helped me to understand the meaning of Fatima and other such historical places where poor and simple children have been chosen to receive extraordinary graces, and thus become messengers to thousands of others far richer than they in human capacities and earthly goods. Subsequently, I spent a month of vacation for two consecutive summers at La Merci, a new community that l'Arche had begun in the Cognac region of France. While doing graduate studies in spirituality at the Institut Catholique in Paris, I kept in close contact with l'Arche for a year and a half, and then went to Trosly to live there for the final year and a half of my stay in France.

My primary concern during these years of study in Europe was the question of community, in particular, Christian community. I soon became aware that I could learn far more about this subject from a venture like l'Arche than from any amount of reading and discussion. My interest turned more and more in this direction, and the openness and love of the people at l'Arche drew me further into the heart of its life.

I soon came to realize just what a unique community this is – not only with regard to its way of responding to the needs of men and women with developmental disabilities, but especially its response to critical issues that many people face today as individuals, families, and communities of all kinds. L'Arche, it seems to me, is a much-needed message for our times. This message cannot be adequately translated into words, but it is of sufficient depth and importance that even an inadequate translation can be helpful. This latter conviction encouraged me to attempt this book, to enable others to experience this community and its message, at least vicariously.

Jean Vanier's own words give us a first glimpse of what the message of l'Arche is all about. (Unless otherwise indicated, the quotations of Jean Vanier are from various unpublished conferences given at Trosly and elsewhere.)

> More and more the world seems to be dividing itself into two. On the one hand there are those motivated by the accumulation of riches, by the need to possess, and by the need to dominate and be above others. On the other hand there are those who live in involuntary poverty and misery and who are in some way marginal to society (the aged, the handicapped of all kinds, the alcoholics, the mentally ill, and so forth, and those who live in misery in the developing countries). Is not the great challenge of the day to create communities which by their joy and simplicity of life draw the "rich" towards a life of greater simplicity and self-gift, and that draw the miserable towards a new hope? Are not these new type of communities (which in fact are quite ancient since they resemble the first Christian communities) a great means of bringing a solution to the suffering, the war, and the revolutions so prevalent in our times? When the distance between the society seeking domination and possession, and the miserable masses living in poverty, becomes too great, we can be sure that one day a spark will ignite the explosion. Do we not need communities of those who choose poverty, happy to share their lives with the rejected in order to create a bridge between the two worlds?

Joy and simplicity certainly do characterize the prevailing spirit of l'Arche. It was this spirit that first struck me upon arriving there. Visitors are almost invariably touched by this experience, and many write letters of thanks that express something of what they have received there.

The mother of one of the assistants wrote from Canada after having spent a week at l'Arche, "I find it very hard to put into words what is in my heart. My visit to your little village of Trosly will always remain one of the most rewarding experiences of my life."

The superior of a group of nuns who spent a weekend there wrote, "The Sisters have absorbed there a climate of intelligent and total charity, of respect for others, that has done them an immense good."

A helicopter pilot in Korea wrote to a friend he had visited briefly at l'Arche. It is interesting to note how, many months later, individual people and their expressions are what remained dear to him:

> I got the very greatest newsletter from Mr. Vanier last month. It touched my cold heart to read of the happy progress made at Trosly, and I took particular delight in remembering favorite names like René (of course), Bernard, le Père, Alain, Danielle, Michel, Abdullah – who was baptized at Carlepont. But what is the name of the philosopher, a champion, who said at Le Val Fleuri: "*Un autre mort, merde!*"

A seventeen-year-old lad from Amiens, having passed several weeks at l'Arche, wrote,

> Having arrived home from my all-too-brief stay at Trosly, I would like to express all the joy and contentment that I experienced there. It seems to me that your community represents an oasis of joy and simplicity in our world.

These letters are typical of the comments made by the many visitors who pass through l'Arche. The final letter that I am going to cite (at some length) is less typical, not so much because of its contents, but because of the circumstances. The author had no previous knowledge of l'Arche; he merely stopped there for a day and a half because a friend of his was there. He is a member of the Communist Party in Canada, an engineer by profession, who had a few months previously left his firm to come to Europe in search of a more meaningful way of life. After two fruitless months of searching, he happened to stop at Trosly to visit his friend. A week after his departure, he wrote to this friend,

After my hurried departure from the peaceful village of Trosly, I felt a little ungrateful to have omitted thanking with words and gestures all those who made possible my stay in that veritable kingdom of Goodness and who each contributed in his own way to make it so pleasant for me…. I only wish all of them could have read in the depths of my heart all the gratitude that I did not know how to express…. I have lived at Trosly hours of interior peace that no sum of money could ever have gained for me…. My stay in Frankfurt has been really most peaceful. I arrived there Friday noon and until my departure at eleven o'clock this morning I passed the major part of my time meditating and pondering over the experience I had lived out at Trosly. It is now several months since I left Montreal to escape the artificiality and to try to unearth in some corner of the world a little human warmth. I certainly never dreamed that I would have to traverse thousands of miles to have any chance of success and I was far from suspecting that in a little village of France perhaps not unlike villages in Quebec, I would find the treasure I was seeking. As Jean Vanier said so well, the fellows of Trosly are "the super-endowed with love." At Frankfurt I was trying to figure out how I could be one of them while at the same time assuming my responsibilities and accepting to be logical. Is this harmony possible? Will it finally fade away? The future will tell….

It was only after I had been there for several weeks that I began to see that, besides the joy, a tremendous amount of suffering is also an essential element in the spirit of l'Arche. For many months this question of joy and suffering was brewing within me almost without my realizing it. Then, one bright spring day at Trosly as I gazed out the window of my little room, I saw something that suddenly illuminated this question and gave me a key to a better understanding of this community.

There in the garden beneath my window were two people at play: one a stunningly beautiful young woman, the other a man with a severe disability. L'Arche is as simple as two people at play in a garden, but for all its simplicity, it has a truly revolutionary message.

Myriam, a lovely young woman with much talent and a winning personality, chooses to spend her afternoons with Denis, who, from all outward appearances, possesses little that is attractive. Many would consider him to be unappealing in his sullenness, with his pursed features, and without sufficient awareness to blow his constantly running nose. Denis speaks very little, and when he does, his words are usually violent. He has just come to l'Arche for a trial period. If all goes well, he will come back on a permanent basis when there is room for him. His background had evidently created in him a deep anguish and anger. Denis, like so many others, is the victim of a whole network and history of rejection and aggression. He has lived in a society that has made it impossible for his parents to simply love and accept him as the gift that he is, a society that in many subtle and not so subtle ways has been telling him and those around him that he never should have been conceived, or at least he should have been destroyed while still in his mother's womb. Little wonder, then, that he is filled with fear, anguish, and anger. In some ways, Myriam's role is to put a stop to this chain of violence by responding to Denis's anguish with love and compassion rather than anger and aggression. She is present to him as a source of peace that can draw out and absorb some of his anguish.

But she does not do this as an act of stoic heroism. When I spoke with Myriam about her relationship to Denis, she smiled gently and said how wonderful he is and how much she appreciated his company. Evidently, she refused to be put off by his not so attractive exterior, and had drawn close enough to perceive something of the inner riches of his person – a person she tries to call forth into greater fullness and vitality. It is an act of contemplation by which one is still and open enough to penetrate beyond the exterior of things so as to touch something of the hidden mystery of reality. Denis, on the other hand, in virtue of his very vulnerability and human poverty, calls Myriam forth into greater fullness and vitality. While he may threaten people who remain at a distance, Myriam has come close enough to sense the trembling and vulnerable person who desperately needs her love. In the face of such a defenseless person she, too, can let down some of her own defenses and be much more open and transparent, much more her true self. In her relationship with Denis, Myriam is aware that each encounter has the potential to call him forth to greater life, to allow him to remain where he is, or to force him further into the death of loneliness and isolation. In this kind of relationship with the weak and defenseless, we become aware of the way that all personal relationships are a matter of life and death. Thus l'Arche offers an extraordinary opportunity to learn that each encounter with each and every person is an important moment – a moment in which to call others forth, give them life, or in some way leave them in the death of their loneliness or self-doubt.

The challenge to the people of l'Arche to become sources of peace for one another gives birth to a twofold movement: a movement toward interiority, toward deepening the wellsprings of peace within oneself in order to be more of a source of peace for others; and an outward movement toward a world steeped in violence and in dire need of people and communities of peace. Jean Vanier speaks of the need for a "revolution of love and compassion" to stem the tide of violence and division. His community is, he hopes, a humble but real contribution to this revolution.

Vanier feels, and his community may indeed verify, that the peaceful revolution that alone can save humankind from destroying itself with the aggression of competition and the violence of self-defense is primarily an affair of the heart and an issue of community. (He explores this way to peace in his book *Finding Peace*, published in 2003.) Peace is, of course, the responsibility of us all, but we tend to think that it belongs especially to national and world leaders in the domains of politics, business, science, and religion. However, these leaders are themselves caught in the dynamics of the power struggle of competition and defensiveness that leaves little hope for creative transformation. So perhaps the greatest hope lies not in a transformation structured from without by political and economic measures or authoritative pronouncements, but from within, by people who have experienced or at least sensed that there is an alternative to the path along which humankind is presently rushing toward self-destruction. Communities such as l'Arche, where the victims or "rejects" of society find the opportunity to be themselves and make their gifts to the world, are living proof that an alternative exists.

The classic image of the beginning of the human person's separation from God and so from the self is that of the man and woman in the Garden of Eden who refuse to accept their state of dependence. My watching a man and a woman at play in a garden becomes symbolic of the revolution back toward that lost unity. In Myriam and Denis we see the symbol of all that an individualistic and competitive society might claim as reasons for their having nothing to do with one another – the woman's attractiveness and talent, the man's apparent lack of any beauty and talent. But Myriam and Denis (rich and poor, joyful and suffering) interact as brother and sister. And they are at play – symbolic of freedom, of going beyond death with childlike confidence in the Creator and Sustainer of life.

But l'Arche is no Garden of Eden. Life there is fraught with difficulties and much suffering. Many a person at Trosly or in the newer communities in France, India, and North America, weighed down by some particular burden or simply by the dull monotony of daily existence, are tempted to give it all up. Some, in fact, do just that. Others, however, are restored by the understanding eyes of a Raphaël or an Isabel who, transcending their own frustrations of not being able to marry or not being able to speak, can, with a mere look, express much love and compassion for a weary friend. Or they may be re-created, as I so often was, by someone like my friend Claude.

Claude had the most illogical mind I had ever encountered. He would ask such questions as "What time is orange?" or "How was tomorrow?" – but he had a wisdom all his own. As a result of his lack of logic he did many things wrong, so he suffered considerably from a kind of constant abuse that he had to endure. Yet Claude was marvelously resilient and kept bouncing back joyfully. For those who discovered his "music," his unique way of responding to life, he was a source of much joy. One day Claude was at the beach with Jean-Pierre and several others of the Ambleteuse community (near Boulogne). The ocean was at low tide, exposing an immense stretch of flat, sandy beach. The group began making designs in the sand. Claude drew a big circle with a couple of marks inside that could have been facial features. "What's that?" asked Jean-Pierre. With a big smile Claude replied, "It's Madame Sun." "That's good," Jean-Pierre said. "Now let's see you draw joy." Claude took a look around him at the wide beach that stretched out in both directions as far as the eye could see, turned to Jean-Pierre and said with a huge smile, but in all seriousness, "There's not enough room!"

It is especially individuals like Claude, men and women who are deeply wounded, people who have been rejected by the world of "normality," who can speak a message of hope to that world. L'Arche is giving these people the chance to be themselves and make their contributions to society. While technological society, with its values of competition and success, borders on despair, communities of l'Arche are beginning to blossom. These communities, with their Claudes and their Isabels, are telling us that there remains in this world enough room for joy, and they point the way to finding it.

2

The Launching

O, Marie, nous vous demandons de bénir notre maison
Gardez-la dans votre coeur immaculé
Faites de l'Arche notre vrai foyer…

We were at the evening prayer around the dinner table. The table had been cleared and the dishes washed. Three candles, spaced out on the long table, were the only source of light in the room. Their flickering light was enough to show the glowing faces of Raphaël, Maxime, Jacques, Jean, Zizi, Benoit, Joan, Louise, and a few of the others seated around the table. We numbered about 14 that night. The long, angular face of Jean Vanier radiated a deep peacefulness. Then only in his mid-40s, Vanier, by his ceaseless efforts and concern for others, had taken on the appearance of a much older man – a man of wisdom.

Many had been at the community Mass earlier that evening. I know Maxime was there, as I saw him still in the chapel sometime after the Mass. He always remained to make his thanksgiving, during which time, as he said, he would sing canticles in his heart to express his gratitude and listen to Jesus, who spoke to him in his heart. I had concelebrated the Mass with Père Thomas, the saintly Dominican priest whom l'Arche was fortunate to have as its co-founder and chaplain. The sermons of this retired philosophy professor revealed something of his Thomistic background. They were words to challenge the most intelligent minds and the most profound spirits, but words delivered with a warmth and simplicity that held the attention of even the most limited listeners. As I stepped outside from that modest but oddly charming and prayerful chapel and closed the door behind me, only the cross on the door distinguished it from the other gray stone village houses.

Then, in early November, it was already dark at seven in the evening. Across the village square I could just make out the form of what used to be the town's only hotel, now La Grande Source, a l'Arche place of welcome. I could hear Maxime moving quickly away down the street. It was too dark to see him, but I recognized the dragging foot of his paralyzed right side, and the enthusiastic, if not too melodious, singing that expressed something of his inner joy. I followed him down the street past the bistro where some of the men of the village were gathered for their evening chat over a few glasses of wine, past the little stone houses that have been standing here for centuries, their closed shutters hiding the simple and hardy people beginning their evening meal. A couple of the houses were more familiar to me. Here, Madame Cagniard had lived with her son and daughter-in-law. She used to do the laundry in the Val Fleuri, one of the l'Arche residences, and her daughter-in-law did most of the housekeeping. There was the Pigeonnier, where eight or ten of the women assistants roomed, and next to it the Sénevé, which housed five or six more.

Finally, I caught up with Maxime. He extended his healthy left hand in greeting and gave me a big smile: "*Bonsoir, mon Père.*" While we exchanged a few words, Maxime continued humming and singing. After the Mass he could not contain his joy. So together we arrived at the little house at the end of the street. The simple wooden plaque over the door was visible thanks to the welcoming lamp above it: "L'Arche."

As we stepped inside from the cold November evening, we were greeted by warmth, light, the smell of good cooking, and joyful voices, all of which blended into the overall impression of "home." I joined those who were relaxing in the living room. Roger was smoking a cigarette. Jim was reading, as usual. Benoit, in front of the radio, was bouncing up and down in time to the music. Zizi was writing and conferring with Pierrot for the next issue of the *Trosly-Potin*, l'Arche's weekly newspaper (four or five mimeographed pages, circulation 85, price 10 centimes). Judging from their laughter, it was not going to be a very serious edition, which would surprise no one. Joan was knitting. Raphaël came in, gave me a big smile, and began mumbling and gesticulating. While I was trying to decipher his message, Louise, in the other room, rang a little cow bell, and called, "*À table!*"

The readiness with which we began moving through the little hallway into the dining room indicated how hungry we were. The volume of talking and laughing mounted steadily as others arrived from their rooms upstairs or came in the front door, which opened onto the dining room. The decor of the house was very simple: stone tile floors, no rugs, some photos and pictures hanging on the papered walls, cheap but colorful printed drapes on the windows. An oil stove heated the living room, and another, the dining room.

We found our places around the table by finding the napkin ring with our name – a simple process, since the places usually didn't vary that much. The paper napkins were for the guests, of which there were several this evening, invited from the other houses; this swelled our number to over 20. It was crowded, but no one seemed to mind. Everyone was obviously used to this sort of thing.

Jean Vanier's napkin ring at an empty place in the middle indicated that he would arrive sooner or later. Louise handed the Bible to Jacques. As he leafed through it searching for a text, the room became a bit quieter. Pierrot continued to banter with Philippe, and Raphaël was still trying to tell me something by repeating in his mumbling way what sounded like "*pas là.*" Then Jacques made the sign of the cross and others followed suit. In his boyish voice Jacques read a brief passage of the gospel, flawlessly pronouncing each word and phrase. After a moment of silence, Pierrot began singing grace. We all joined in enthusiastically. By the last phrase most of us have gotten the right key. There was a scraping of chairs until everyone sat down; Louise began serving up the steaming soup. The bantering and laughing picked up immediately. Three or four conversations were going all at once. Raphaël again tried to get through to me: "*Pas là.*" "Who is not here?" I asked. Pointing to himself with an almost violent gesture he grunted what I had come to recognize as the word "*moi.*" So Raphaël would not be here, but when? More gestures and mumbling, which I couldn't understand. But Lucien, who had been at l'Arche almost as long as Raphaël and the other "founding fathers," Pierrot and Philippe, was able to help. After a couple of guesses he said, "Saturday," and Raphaël smiled and nodded in agreement. "But where are you going?" I continued. In response he gave me a military salute. Then I was distracted as Véronique, to my left, asked me if I could reach the soup and serve up another bowl to Jacques. A couple of others passed their soup plates as well.

Finally, turning back to Raphaël, I saw that he was trying to explain the same message to Barbara. I could now be of some help, since I had deciphered the first half of the message: "He says he won't be here to eat on Saturday." And so Raphaël nodded and began to salute again. "You're going to visit your friend the army chaplain?" I suggested, but it was not that. "You're going to do your military service," someone said, but he shook his head. Then Barbara, who had known Raphaël since her arrival at Trosly shortly after l'Arche was founded, explained, "It's Camille, the brother of Anne-Marie." Anne-Marie, a young woman of the village, was doing the cooking here; and her brother Camille was doing his military service. Raphaël was one great smile as he nodded in assent. "Anne-Marie has invited you to eat with them Saturday evening?" Barbara continued. Raphaël finally relaxed back in his chair and smiled contentedly, giving us all a look that said, "It was perfectly obvious what I was trying to say; what took you so long to understand?"

Meanwhile, Pierrot had been at his favorite pastime of kidding Zizi. Although he claimed to have had his fill of Canadians, he got along famously with this young French Canadian who was taking a year off from her studies to work at l'Arche. "Sha ta," he said with a big toothy grin, trying out some of his newly acquired English. We had come to recognize this expression, which was supposed to be "shut up."

The front door opened, and the tall figure of Jean Vanier stepped quietly into the room. He was slightly stooped from years of bending to give his full attention to smaller people. He smiled and bowed in a gesture of humble apology, while a clatter of happy voices went up in mock protest.

Raphaël grunted what we all knew to be the words "Too late! Too late!" Pierrot exclaimed, "No excuses! No excuses!" While Marie-Elizabeth quickly went to the kitchen for some hot soup, Jean took his place at the table, manifesting great contentment to be with his family. Simply and unpretentiously he turned all of his attention first to Jacques, then to Benoit, to George, Louise, and so on, calling forth each of them to be more a part of the entire gathering.

Thus the meal proceeded in a cheerful atmosphere. Most people seemed very much at home, but some, like George, were quiet and exchanged only a few whispered words with their neighbor. Benoit responded mechanically and briefly to questions that were put to him, but was otherwise occupied with his food and his own thoughts, which sometimes caused him to smile broadly or other times to strike himself sharply on the cheek. At the end of each course in the meal, a few people got up without a word, took the soup pot or serving dishes back to the kitchen, and brought in the next course.

Several baskets of fruit were carried in for dessert. Someone had put a plastic banana in with the oranges and pears. Most of us spotted it immediately and exchanged knowing smiles. The basket was offered to Philippe, who loved bananas. He reached quickly for his favorite fruit but as soon as he touched it he knew he had been had. "*Merde!*" he shouted as everyone burst into laughter, especially Raphaël, who all but fell off his chair, which provoked even more laughter.

When the meal was finally finished we all stood and joined in as Pierrot began a rousing song of thanksgiving.

There was a race for the kitchen to see who would get to the sink first and thus wash the dishes. Jean quickly stretched out his long arm and held back Marie-Elizabeth in order to step in front of her. But Véronique was closer to the door to the kitchen. Jean raced after her. As Véronique went around the kitchen table, which blocked the way to the sink, Jean leaped over it and landed at the sink before her.

Véronique screamed with excitement and the shock of almost being trapped under this immense form descending from above. Jean burst out laughing as he rolled up his sleeves and filled the sink. Everyone helped to clear the table and do the dishes. Jacques rinsed, and Raphaël slowly handed the dishes to be dried to those waiting patiently, or not so patiently, with their dish towels. It would have gone more quickly if Raphaël had not been there, but each time he handed out a dripping plate it was accompanied by a look of such friendship that no one could regret the extra few minutes. The little kitchen was a scene of happy chaos.

When the dishes were done, most of us returned to the dining room for the evening prayer. As usual, Philippe suggested that we not delay too long with the prayer so that he wouldn't miss the start of the film or whatever the program happened to be on TV (although watching TV was a rare event there). That evening, at Jean's request, Maxime led the prayer. He began by asking if anyone had any particular intentions. Pierre, beside me, had just whispered that he was very sad in thinking of his mother, who had died the previous year, and his father, who had died the year before. It was the day following All Souls' Day. I suggested that we pray for Pierre and his departed parents. After a moment's silence, Jacques took this theme up, and spoke of how he felt when he was young and his parents died. He said, "It was extremely hard, and I didn't want to believe it when they told me my mother had died, and I refused to go and look at her body." After a pause he continued, "Yes, it's tough at the beginning, but you sooner or later get accustomed to it – and they are happy in heaven, and that's the most important thing."

This time of prayer was a privileged moment of truth, when people would express their deepest feelings, feelings they might never dare to express in another context. For instance, one evening when each one was saying what aspect of Jesus and his life meant most to us, Pierrot said that, for him, it was how Jesus gave sight to the blind man. Then he continued by telling us that his own father was losing his eyesight.

So now Jacques invited Maxime to speak: "And you, Maxime, do you have any intentions?" Maxime suggested that we pray for Gabrielle and Ron, who were at that time in India. Yes, said Jacques, and especially for those poor and lonely people who come and find refuge at Asha Niketan (the name given to the l'Arche home in India, a phrase meaning Home of Hope). Then Joan, a young woman from Toronto who had been at l'Arche since the summer, said in her less than perfect French that we could pray for Regina, who would be leaving Thursday to join the others in India. Silence. Then Bruno, who was always up on current events, said something about the youths recently killed in a dance-hall fire in southern France, suggesting that we pray for those who had died and for their families. Quietly Jean began to speak of his concern for one of the newly established homes elsewhere in France. The young couple in charge there was feeling fragile and in need of the support of our prayers. Then, in great simplicity, he spoke to Jesus in a way that made me feel deeply the presence of this unseen friend.

After a long silence, Pierrot began singing the Our Father and all joined in. Raphaël, too, with undistinguishable sounds and no recognizable tune, added what he could to the singing. It was followed immediately by the l'Arche prayer, "O Marie, nous vous demandons":

Mary, we ask you to bless our house.
Keep it safe in your immaculate heart.
Make l'Arche our true home,
a refuge for the poor in spirit,

that they may find here the Source of all life,
a refuge for those who are severely tried,
that they may be ceaselessly consoled.
Mary, give us hearts that are humble and gentle
to welcome with kindness and compassion
all those whom you send to us.
Give us hearts full of mercy to love them, to serve them, to
extinguish all discord
and to see in our suffering brother the living presence of
Jesus.
Lord, bless us from the hand of your poor.
Lord, smile on us through the eyes of your poor.
Lord, receive us one day in the holy company of your poor.
Amen.

Then Pierrot whispered, "*Notre-Dame de l'Arche, priez pour nous!*" (Our Lady of l'Arche, pray for us!), to which all responded quietly, "Amen."

"*Notre-Dame de Lourdes, priez pour nous!*" "Amen."

Maxime continued, "*Notre-Dame de l'Inde* [India], *priez pour nous!*" "Amen."

"*Notre-Dame de l'Aurore* [for l'Arche Daybreak in Canada], *priez pour nous!*" "Amen."

"*Notre-Dame de la paix* [peace], *priez pour nous!*" "Amen."

Silence, and then Pierrot began a hymn to the Blessed Virgin and all joined in, including Raphaël. Finally, a deep silence enveloped everyone, while the candles flickered in the darkness. A profound sense of peace and unity pervaded the room. It held us all breathlessly still for a couple of minutes, then Maxime made the sign of the cross. Others followed. Jacques leaned over the table to blow out the candles; Zizi tried to blow them out before he could. Someone turned on the lights. Raphaël, getting to his feet, dropped his pipe, which evoked the one word he could say with perfect clarity: "*Merde.*"

Jean began saying goodnight to each one, taking their hand and looking intently and lovingly into their eyes. A few people moved into the living room to relax, listen to records, read or write letters. Pierre challenged Roger to a game of chess. Raphaël came to me and asked if I would perform the wedding ceremony for him and whatever girl happened to be nearby; that night it was Joan. Since it was a Tuesday, Maxime got his coat to return to the chapel. A couple of others, after saying goodnight and shaking hands with everyone, slipped out and headed for the chapel, too. Lucien was already in his room listening to his records. The sounds of a Bach organ recital wafted down the stairs.

Jean quickly caught up with Philippe, took him by the arm and proceeded down the road with him. Jean was going to his office, where until late into the night he would be engaged with a bit of paperwork, but mostly with members of the community coming to see him on business or for personal guidance. So the evening drew to an end peacefully, as they generally had since Jean Vanier settled here a number of years ago. A vaguely similar evening had been spent in the other homes that had been opened in Trosly in the intervening years.

Perhaps "peaceful" was not the word to describe the Val Fleuri, the largest of the homes. With so many living in "the Val," it is almost too large to be called a home. However, anyone partaking in a meal in this great old chateau could not help but be touched by the warmth and joyfulness of the atmosphere. The Val Fleuri is where it all began.

In 1960, Mr. Pratt, the father of Jean-Pierre, a lad with a developmental disability, and Dr. Préaut, who had many years of professional experience in the field, began the Val Fleuri as a residence and workshop for Jean-Pierre and other such young men. They invited Père Thomas Philippe to come to Trosly as the chaplain because they wanted this home to have a religious orientation. As Père Thomas saw it, these two men invited him to come precisely as a chaplain, "as a poor instrument who could help individuals live more fully in the Holy Spirit." It was clear right from the beginning, he noted, that here at Trosly there would be given this special orientation of helping each person to develop an interior life, more and more illuminated and guided by the Holy Spirit.

A year later, at the urging of Père Thomas, Jean Vanier's friend and former tutor, Vanier came to Trosly. It marked for him the end of a long search and the beginning of an extraordinary and unsuspected career.

Jean Vanier was born in 1928, the son of Pauline and Georges Vanier, who was a distinguished soldier and later Governor General of Canada. Jean seemed destined, from a very early age, to follow his father in a military career. Robert Speaight notes, in his biography of General Vanier, that in 1942,

> Jock (as Jean is called by his family) had passed into the Royal Naval College, Dartmouth [England], now removed to Eaton Hall in Cheshire. A report described him as having no great gifts in the way of brains or athletic ability, but he is a very likeable character and should do well in the long run. In view of his subsequent achievements this was an understatement wholly in keeping with the traditions of the Royal Navy.[1]

At the age of 20, Jean was already an officer on Canada's only aircraft carrier. His mother remembered her husband's response to a report he had received concerning his son, then a student at Dartmouth. The report noted that Jean showed some good qualities for an officer but that he lacked respect for his senior officers. "As long as he never shows a lack of respect for those under him, he'll be all right," the general responded happily. At that time, of course, he had no idea of the great respect and concern that his son was to acquire for the weakest and most defenseless members of society.

Eventually it became clear to Jean that God had other things in mind for him than the concerns of an aircraft carrier. (This ship was later sold for scrap, while Jean Vanier's fragile little Ark shows signs of staying afloat for some time to come.) Jean reflects that when he found himself reciting the divine office instead of attending to the night watch it became evident that this was not his place. In 1950 he resigned his commission with the Royal Canadian Navy.

Thus began a long period of searching. He made enquiries into several different lay communities that, in one way or another, were concerned with living the gospel in a spirit of poverty. One such community, of which he had some slight knowledge, was Eau Vive in France. The response to his enquiry about this community, a letter from its founder and director, Père Thomas Philippe, convinced him to go there, even though he had come across several other interesting possibilities. Eau Vive was a community of students in a poor suburb of Paris, next to the Dominican Priory of the Sauchoir. Its purpose was to give to its members a deeper commitment to their Christian faith by training them in prayer and metaphysics. At the time of Jean's arrival it was home to about 80 students. A year later, due to a complexity of issues, including poor health, Père Thomas was forced to give up the direction of Eau Vive. It is an indication of the respect that Père Thomas had for Jean that he should hand over the direction to him, after only one year's acquaintance with this former naval officer who was over 20 years his junior.

This change in leadership precipitated a crisis in Eau Vive's relationship with the Sauchoir. The Dominicans had considered Eau Vive to be under their jurisdiction, and so were unhappy that its direction should be taken over by a layman. The doors of the Sauchoir were closed to the members of Eau Vive. Denied the opportunity of studying with the Dominicans and the use of their library, many students left Eau Vive; only 25 or so remained. Most of these pursued their studies at the Institut Catholique, also in Paris. Still, Eau Vive managed to survive this crisis and continue for six or seven more years, with Vanier at its helm.

Meanwhile, Jean Vanier had been accepted as a candidate to the priesthood for the diocese of Quebec, with the blessing of the bishop to continue his studies in Europe. Shortly before he was to return to Quebec to prepare for the subdiaconate, a new crisis arose at Eau Vive. The local bishop was forced to ask Jean and the other leaders to resign and to sign a statement of submission to church authority. Jean recalls that the bishop was embarrassed to the point of confusion, so much so that he inadvertently handed

Jean the wrong statement: a declaration of refusal to submit to the church! (An event ten years later offers a striking contrast to this episode. The 10,000 people who happened to be in St. Peter's Basilica for the Wednesday audience prior to Pentecost could have had no doubt that Jean Vanier was a loyal son of the church. Jean was there that day with some 200 members of the communities from Trosly and La Merci on pilgrimage to the Eternal City. As he went up on the dais and was presented to Pope Paul VI, the two men warmly embraced each other in a sign of mutual love and respect. Later Jean had similar tender moments of encounter with John Paul II.)

The dismissal from Eau Vive left Vanier in a state of uncertainty not unlike that of seven years earlier, when he had resigned from the Navy. He decided against entering the major seminary to complete his final year of preparation for the priesthood.

He lived for the next few years with little or no experience of community. One year was spent boarding at the Trappist monastery of Bellefontaine in France; another, on a small farm he had purchased and where, in his own words, he "lived very much alone." During a year spent in Rome he continued some private studies in theology with Père Thomas. One of the last of these years of searching was spent in a little cottage at Fatima, which he had purchased some years earlier in the hope that it might be the location for a new community of Eau Vive. In 1962 he successfully defended his doctorate in philosophy at the Institut Catholique in Paris, and then joined the faculty of St. Michael's College, University of Toronto, to begin a part-time teaching career.

That same year, Père Thomas had become the chaplain of Val Fleuri. A year or so later, encouraged by Père Thomas, Jean came to Trosly, where he bought a dilapidated old house, christened it "l'Arche" and launched it on August 5, 1964.

Looking back on the years that preceded the founding of l'Arche, Jean Vanier feels that his six years in the community of Eau Vive were the "most formative of these long years of searching – even far more than the actual studies pursued." He had come to the conviction that he was called to form community, with some of the poor and rejected of society. Jean says that in moving into his little house with Raphaël and Philippe, he was sure of only one thing. In taking these men out of the institutions to which they had been condemned and bringing them to l'Arche, he was making an irrevocable move. He had no idea whether there would be other people willing to come and help him, but he did know that he was committed to live with these two men for the rest of his life or theirs.

His decision caused considerable consternation among his family and friends, who could not understand this sacrifice of a most promising academic career for a seemingly worthless alternative. However, Jean knew that this was something he had to do in response to a call that was too clear to deny or ignore.

There was no glamour, no clear plan or vision for the future, in moving into a ramshackle house in an out-of-the-way corner of the world with two lonely and rejected men. This simple, concrete gesture was the thing at hand to be done, and Jean did it. It was this gesture that sowed the seed for all that continues to flourish, directly or indirectly, from Jean's inspiration, like a fulfillment of the words of the Gospel: "Unless a grain of wheat falls into the ground and dies, it remains alone; but if it dies, it bears much fruit" (John 12:24).

3

Setting the Course

L'Arche has taken on dimensions far beyond the expectations Jean Vanier held when he opened his little home in the summer of '64. He says that his original idea was to create "a home of mercy where the rejects of society could find refuge and where they would be welcomed with kindness and compassion." However, after a month or two living with Raphaël and Philippe, he began to formulate a very different vision.

Out of the commitment to live with these men came the discovery of their gifts and potential. Jean noticed, for example, how Philippe was making a slide collection with which to entertain his friends. Raphaël would save the many wooden matches he used each day to light his pipe and take them to a little boy down the street to play with. He would hide away chocolates and other such gifts so he might later share them with others. Before long, he had become the friend of many in the village, especially the children and the elderly, who had no problem with Raphaël's almost complete inability to speak. These two men had both the need and the capacity to give to others. Jean came to realize that if people with developmental disabilities "are given a good human situation in which to live and are sustained by loving relationships, they are capable of progressing in an astonishing way on the psychological, human, and spiritual planes."

Along with this discovery came an event that also widened the scope of l'Arche. Three months after Jean had settled in the town of Trosly, there was a crisis in the direction of the Val Fleuri. The Val Fleuri comprised a large residence (the old village chateau) and sheltered workshops (the chateau stables) for about 20 young men with disabilities. Jean was asked to take over its direction. A doctorate in philosophy had scarcely prepared him for such a venture, but with the strong encouragement of Père Thomas he accepted the position.

He can now laugh at the way he practiced on an orange before giving his first hypodermic needle to a very agitated young man. Besides learning how to give medical help to the residents, he was also learning about the nature of their suffering. As he says, "Since their infancy almost all of them have been wounded not only organically but by so many looks of pity, disdain, and indifference that have made them feel worthless and inferior and have destroyed any confidence they may have had in themselves." So what they most needed was to be loved and accepted as people.

Vanier needed others who would be willing to live with the men on this level of acceptance and friendship. In response to Vanier's invitation as he spoke of his work to people in France and in Canada (where he continued to lecture on a part-time basis), men and women began to arrive – like Henri, who came from the north of France and stayed for many years, and Barbara, from Buffalo, who never left. Others, like Steve and Anne, Agnes and Adriano, came for a while and then moved on to start other l'Arche communities. Many came for the summer months or longer periods as a break from studies or other work. Those who came quickly began to discover the riches of Raphaël, Philippe, and the others. Anne-Marie, a student from Quebec, observed, "Raphaël brings me so much – his smile is extraordinary." David, a college graduate from Ontario, took awhile but finally appreciated Raphaël:

He's such a genuine person. I couldn't understand this until last Saturday when I went to say goodbye to everybody. I walked out to my car, and Raphaël was standing over near the fence just a bit from my car. So I went over to say goodbye to him and explain to him that I was leaving – and all of a sudden – just the look in his eyes, the sadness, the real feeling of genuine sadness. He said: "*Pas pars*," you can't leave, you have to stay and work. Just a simple statement, but for me at the point it was just too much. That was the first time that I felt that I had communicated with him. And just to watch his eyes then. I understand now what people mean because he has such an open spirit, he accepts people so beautifully. There's a communication problem, too. You have to know Raphaël pretty well in order to be able to communicate with him. It took me quite awhile to beam in on his sort of communication. The other night I was back there to see Mary and Judy and he was standing outside Mary and Judy's room. And he turned to his right and saw these flowers that were blooming on a bush, and he said they were very beautiful: "*Elles poussent bien.*" And then he turned to his left and there were some of those little snowdrop flowers and they were all dead. And you could just see the change in his eyes from the joy when he looked at the live flowers to the sadness when he saw the dead ones. It was beautiful.

While people came with many different motives, almost invariably they were surprised at how much they received. For Diane and Helen, it was "just a way to pass the summer." Yet to their delight, it was a "very, very beautiful experience – we had such terrific friends among these guys."

Tom, a schoolteacher, reflects, "I don't think I had any particularly humanitarian motives…. I was interested and now I'm even more interested." He concludes, "It's like living in a very big family – which is great." Dave, a graduate student in theology, observes, "Really, you come here thinking you want to serve, help out where you can, but you get more out of it than you can possibly give."

Pierre came from a nearby city in France. He had a clear idea of why he came there: "I came first of all because I plan to go into the profession of special education, and secondly to experience real community life." He goes on to say, "I think these guys have given me much more than I expected." Anne-Marie says, "I was afraid I wouldn't be able to accept this kind of person, but I discovered that they are great – they humanize us a great deal."

As people came and were so obviously enriched by living there, it became more and more evident that l'Arche was not just a place of refuge. It was a community where all could progress together toward greater wholeness. If it was not to be simply a refuge, neither was it just a place to do nothing but try to be a community. For one thing, there was work to be done. There were the workshops and gardens as well as the maintenance and daily chores of the homes. However, both the work and the community life itself are at the service of the growth and development of the individual. As Vanier sees it, "The aim of this community is not efficiency and productivity, but human and spiritual progress, which ought necessarily to be founded on an openness and mutual respect, and the desire to see the other achieve the greatest possible liberty."

Many experienced this greater liberty, the freedom to be more oneself. The very simplicity of the people with developmental disabilities seems to be a key to opening others and allowing them to be more simple and more truly themselves.

Mary, a nurse, claims: "I could be myself at l'Arche – yes, very much, because one is not threatened, and there is such welcome. They really accept you and make you feel at home." Tom finds his own self more, thanks to the simplicity he met in the individuals who live there:

> I think it's the simplicity of the guys. There's no need of doing a lot – you can't distract them anyway. The relationship that exists between ourselves and the guys is so simple. They don't want a whole bunch of talk, or that you buy anything for them. They're not interested in how bright you are, what degrees you have, what kind of clothes you wear. All they want to do is to take your hand, or have you put your arm around their shoulder, or tell them they're doing a good job, or horse around with them. They don't look for anything but the essentials. When they can't verbalize, when they can't speak very well, they don't know enough to have all the damn stupid hang-ups we've got. It's just real simple.

Judy, a pre-med student, also speaks of the matter of people being themselves and of accepting others as they are:

L'Arche is such a sincere place. People can be themselves, and it doesn't matter what you were at home, or where you come from, or what degrees you have. I think all the people here have changed – I know I have, in small ways; I know I have very much. And you think now of the people at home, and some of the things that you hear at home, some of the standards on which you judge people, and they are so meaningless now. All that's important is the type of person you are and the type of rapport you can establish with the guys and whether you are sincere or not. On the surface it's a way of looking at people, as they are and not as people say they are. Still, there is something more than this, something deeper. It's largely because of l'Arche that the guys are so rich in spirit. I've met others with developmental disabilities – they have had the same quality, but it's brought out so much at l'Arche. There's always been the same simplicity, but there's never been the same richness. Like when you go to the beach and you see Jean-Claude and René acting up. There's no pretense to them at all. They're real people. They are more real than so many other people I know, who are supposed to have everything. That struck me the first time I saw them in public – it was fantastic. That's what's so wonderful. I don't know if I can – if people can – just be themselves. Not be embarrassed or shy or anything.

The various façades that so many hide behind are much less effective with people with developmental disabilities. They have a way of seeing the person behind the façade, and of relating directly to that person. They are especially sensitive to the suffering of others. It is a common experience at l'Arche for a resident to offer compassion by a look, a word, or a gesture to someone whose suffering is scarcely observable. For example, André spent a few weeks at l'Arche after leaving the monastery where he had lived for a number of years. Few people knew that he was an ex-monk, and even fewer knew of his deep suffering, because he was always laughing. One night at the evening prayer at the Val Fleuri, Patrick, a marvelous man with Down syndrome, said, "Let us pray for André because he is not very happy." He went on to say how sorry he felt for André.

Jean Vanier stated that the aim of l'Arche is not efficiency and productivity. He had been learning from these individuals an alternative to the excessive emphasis that Western society places on efficiency and productivity. It is especially the North Americans who come to l'Arche who are struck by the way different values take precedence there. They speak of how the pace of life has slowed down so that life becomes more enjoyable. There isn't this pressure to accomplish things, concrete things; more concern is given to the people who are doing the job than the job itself. Judy illustrates this point well: "It's when Raphaël wants to help with the potatoes that have to be done by 4:00; so Raphaël helps and they're not done until 4:30 and they're done horribly." Thomas gives an example of how his own attitude has evolved:

> I'll never forget this one thing. We were digging a hole, and it was full of water, and the guy I was working with, Michael, was throwing the water out with a bucket – the most inefficient way of doing it – but he was laughing because the muddy water was splashing up on the trees and the sun was shining through it and it was really pretty, it really looked neat. We just stood there and watched it for about five minutes, and it was really great. That was towards the end of the summer. I would not have enjoyed it at the beginning of the summer because, well, all that water and the hole that we had to get dug. But it was little simple things like that.

The emphasis is on the present moment, enjoying it without being too preoccupied about the future, and so gaining a deeper appreciation for what the moment holds – "just enjoying the afternoon without worrying about what's going to happen tonight and…getting things done at the same time, and enjoying everyone around you." The result is a greater appreciation, not just of people, but also of nature, as Thomas's example indicates, and as he goes on to say, "You appreciate little things more, too, just little things of beauty. I notice myself looking at flowers more, and sunsets. Although I always did like that sort of thing, they've become more important."

David adds that he has gained a deeper appreciation for the basic aspects of life:

> I feel in a sort of undefined way that the definitions for some of the very basic aspects of life have been shaken up or, you know, something like that. What sleep means and what work means and what eating means – it's not what I knew before, and I feel that it's more meaningful. I feel richer in that because I have lived, worked, played, and eaten with the guys.

One aspect of the lifestyle of l'Arche, which until now has been referred to only indirectly, is the means of communication between people. Here I refer not to the passing on of information or instructions, but simply to interpersonal communication. This, of course, is implied in what has been said about a greater appreciation for others, and a greater openness. Some mentioned that the men with disabilities are uninhibited in expressing their affections, even to the point sometimes of "handling you and kissing you and that sort of thing," as one person remarked. Or, as Judy explains, "I think it's fantastic, when I can go downstairs and the guys will be there and they will take you into their arms almost."

But touch is not the only nonverbal communication that is emphasized here. Françoise speaks of the importance of silence itself as a means of personal encounter: "I find that the silence is really extraordinary. People meet one another much more profoundly in silence." She goes on to say how much can be communicated simply by a smile:

> In the workshop there are moments when no one is talking and we are really united. Even by a smile – I find that the smile is very, very important. There is no need for words, but to smile at someone – you touch them much more. It's extraordinary – it's really true. Take Patrick, for example, nothing but a smile, but when he smiles he seems to say, "You know, I really love you." There is something extraordinary there, and nothing has been said. It's extraordinary…. Raphaël doesn't speak very much, but just the same there are quite profound things that happen…. Raphaël has a good gimmick, he's unable to speak.

The openness of the core members also operates on the level of faith, making possible a very simple and direct relationship with God. Many at l'Arche relate to Jesus as to a personal and intimate friend. Prayer and worship are important to them, which surprises many of the more "sophisticated" people who come there – like Donald, a theology student, who spent a summer at l'Arche. He says,

> That was one of the big things that struck me – why the guys were always going to Mass when they were perfectly free to go or not. It was just like a big circus, all that racket and noise – and as I went on, I began to realize that for most of them Mass is a meaningful experience.... Even for Patrick D., the innocent of innocents. It's his best quality. He's incapable of wrong in the moral sense. There is that spiritual part and this has come out from time to time. One time when it came out was when we were having one of those prayer meetings Sunday evening. Everyone was surprised – he just sort of took over. Even for him there's this very spiritual force working. It's not that apparent half the time, but it's apparent that there is some spiritual meaning in the Mass and prayers for him. Another thing that I really liked was the little prayer after dinner. It was kept short, seven to ten minutes, and yet the guys seemed to really enjoy it.

For some, like Brian, this simple faith effected a kind of conversion experience:

> I had kind of forgotten about God. Then, almost without realizing it, here God's presence overwhelmed me and it's almost like coming back to the fold. Where I wanted to question and everything, I realized that it was beyond questioning here and that God was a very real Person because there was nothing else that could make something like this work. And as such I've recognized it in people and what they do – their desire to pray. Because of God's overwhelming presence here it refreshed my mind when it was on the brink of stalemate. Something that struck me with the guys is that – well, young adults always like to question the existence of God and theology and different religions and see what is best for them. Then to see the guys here who just believe, it's almost like blind faith – it's fantastic – it's beyond questioning.

They just accept it and live within it. That is also something that struck me very strongly: this recognition of Christ – when I say Christ, I mean the presence of God.

We can at this point sum up the various qualities of the people at the heart of l'Arche that have been spoken of as a source of inspiration: simplicity of spirit; affection and freedom to genuinely manifest this affection; candidness; openness to life, to people, to God; capacity to make people feel welcome; tendency to be concerned only with the essentials in life and in people; joy and an eagerness to give joy to others; generosity; capacity to live fully the present moment; sense of wonder; sensitivity; unquestioning faith. These positive qualities can be most readily attributed to a child – for adults, they are harder to retain. Clearly, the people who have come to volunteer or work at l'Arche feel that they have been influenced in a positive way by their experience. It has not been simply the experience of serving poor and helpless individuals that is personally enriching, but rather the interpersonal relations with fellow human beings who have much to offer.

It might be useful here to draw into the conversation a psychologist of human relations who might help us to understand what is happening here. Eric Berne, in his bestselling book *Games People Play,* points out that in every person is the Child, the Adult, and the Parent. He goes on to note that "there is no such thing as an 'immature person' – there are only people in whom the Child takes over inappropriately or unproductively."[2]

While noting the importance of the Adult for the survival of the individual, and of the Parent for both the survival of the human race and the conservation of much time and energy by making many responses automatic, Berne nevertheless stresses the importance of the Child to "contribute to the individual's life exactly what an actual child can contribute to family life: charm, pleasure and creativity."[3]

The bulk of his study analyzes the various kinds of games people play as a means of social intercourse that circumvents the threatening relationship of intimacy. Intimacy is the richest form of human relationship, but few people have enough personal autonomy to engage in such relations. The natural Child possesses this autonomy, but rarely resists the parental influence, which tends to destroy it. "The attainment of autonomy," Berne notes, "is manifested by the release or recovery of three capacities: awareness, spontaneity and intimacy."[4]

Spontaneity, as Berne defines it, means "liberation, liberation from the compulsion to play games and have only the feelings one was taught to have."[5] People with developmental disabilities have often been spared from learning the feelings they ought to have. It has been observed how they are free with regards to their feelings. They have little hesitancy in showing both their affection or their disaffection, by either gesture or word. One day, for example, Jean's mother, Madame Vanier, who in the beginning spent a month at Trosly each summer before settling there permanently, invited Michel to come to her home for lunch. She asked him if he would like someone else to join them. "Yes," he said, "Zizi." Madame Vanier discovered, however, that Zizi was not free that day. She then informed Michel that his friend would not be there for lunch. "Well, I'm not coming then," he said. "I don't want to eat with you alone."

Finally, intimacy is defined as the "spontaneous, game-free candidness of an aware person, the liberation of the essentially perceptive, uncorrupted Child in all its naïveté living in the here and now."[6] Candidness is also a quality attributed to the core members at l'Arche. This candidness, Berne notes, is what can evoke affection in others. Those who have lived at l'Arche have, in fact, been drawn into intimacy because of this candidness. Barbara Z., a kind of "American gypsy" who has lived in many parts of the world, wandered into Trosly and stayed for many months. She tells the story of the deep intimacy she experienced there with many, but especially with Ange. One day Barbara was afflicted with diarrhea. She was rushing through the house with the desperate and single-minded intention of getting to the toilet before it was too late. Ange heard her come in and, as she passed his room, in his gentle way he called her name: "Barbara!" She says that, to her own amazement, she stopped at once and went to Ange. (How the episode ended she did not say.)

All this helps us to understand the importance of childlikeness that is stressed in the gospels ("Unless you become as little children you cannot enter the kingdom"), as well as the deep faith that has been attributed to the people at the heart of l'Arche. Childlikeness makes possible an intimate relation with others, as well as with the Other. As Berne says, "Before, unless and until they are corrupted, most infants seem to be loving, and that is the essential nature of intimacy."[7] To a greater degree than most people, men and women with developmental disabilities seem to maintain uncorrupted this capacity for love. People who go to l'Arche are usually touched by the capacity of these people to love on the human level, as well as by their deep, unquestioning faith, and especially by their intimacy with the person of Jesus. As Françoise, a truly radiant young French woman, says,

> It is there that I learned to love and where I received so much. It is not something you learn – it is something you receive. It is not ourselves in any way at all who achieve this. It is God who teaches us – like that – to receive – and our hands like that (open) – that's all.

These qualities of the people Jean Vanier had felt called to help, as well as the way he was seeing them change others who had come to work with him, were making their impact on Jean directly. In proportion to their limitations in the power of reasoning, it seems that people are enriched in the gifts of the heart. These gifts of the heart are precisely what are so greatly needed in a technological society that is becoming ever more heartless. Jean's vision was shifting from a concern for what society could do for individuals with disabilities to a concern for what these individuals could do for society.

Throughout the early years, the community of l'Arche continued to grow. Other houses in Trosly were purchased to begin new homes. As l'Arche grew and became better known, the waiting list of men and women who could no longer be cared for by parents or find adequate accommodations in institutions grew longer. Furthermore, the injustice of confining people in psychiatric hospitals that were little more than prisons was becoming increasingly evident. Jean realized that

> our centre must not be a ghetto where a few people can live happily. We must constantly strive to bring a realistic solution to a human and social problem, that of people with disabilities in our modern society. We would like to see l'Arche become a prototype or model for the creation of other centres and for those who are working for justice in this area.

And so the seeds of new communities started to take root beyond the village of Trosly. Valinos, a center for women, was begun in the nearby town of Cuise-la-Motte. La Merci, a center for men and women, was begun farther south in the Cognac region of France. Then a similar center, called Daybreak, was begun in Canada, just north of Toronto. Asha Niketan opened in Bangalore, India. Finally, in a single year (1972–1973), l'Arche communities were inaugurated in the Canadian cities of Ottawa, Cornwall, Stratford, Edmonton, and Winnipeg, and in Erie (Pennsylvania), Canterbury (England), Copenhagen, Calcutta, and several areas of France.

The establishment of communities in India was especially significant, for it gave Jean a direct contact with the developing world. He found that it was meaningful for the men and women at l'Arche to have their own vision opened to the entire world:

> The opening out of the spirit of our people through their awareness of foundations on other continents will be enormously beneficial to them on the human, cultural, and spiritual plane. Does not human dignity come precisely from this opening out toward the universal?

Indeed, it calls forth in a special way their great capacity for compassion. The prayerful concern that they express for Asha Niketan and all the poor of India is genuine and moving. At various times of the year one of the men at l'Arche, Jacques, takes it upon himself to collect money and send it to Gabrielle for her work in India. This contact with developing countries has deepened Jean's sensitivity to the widening gap between the rich and poor of the world. He began to see l'Arche as a contribution toward bridging this gap.

The faith dimension of this work, evident from the beginning, was gradually being deepened. It was especially the openness to the faith on the part of the more innocent members of the community, cultivated as it was by the attentive ministry of Père Thomas, that was effecting this deepening. Also, it seemed that only by the spirit of the gospel could one continue in this way of life. Jean underlines this fact:

> I have come to realize with ever greater clarity that to live with our people we must be penetrated with the values of the gospel (respect for the human person, especially the most fragile; the primacy of compassion over efficiency and productivity).... Our community implies two aspects: an element of faith, which is central, and a more human element of psychological progress, culture, work, and so forth. It is realized in the profound love which unites us and makes us happy to live together in mutual respect without necessarily practicing the same faith, and in the joy of seeing one another progress in the ways of the Holy Spirit.

This movement was manifested in Vanier's lectures, which were becoming more spiritual in their orientation, more explicitly inspired by the message of the gospel.

In 1968, a group of Catholic priests in Toronto invited Jean to preach a retreat to them. He accepted on the condition that it be not just for priests but for sisters and laypeople, young and old, and people suffering from various physical or developmental disabilities. He also asked that there be a chance for these people to share together in ways that would allow them to enrich one another. The 60 people who made this weeklong experience of "Faith and Sharing" were profoundly touched by it. Thus began a new dimension of Vanier's life. He was beginning to share with many others the gospel message of liberation and hope that he was assimilating in his life at l'Arche. Since that time, he has been taking this message to a widening circle of leaders in society, but especially to the wounded and rejected people themselves. Over the years he has met and spoken to inmates in almost all the major prisons and psychiatric hospitals in Canada. Some years ago, at the request of the prisoners themselves, Jean spent two days in Drumheller prison, Alberta, living in a cell and sharing with the men.

His ever-deepening commitment to work for ecumenical and interfaith dialogue began to take shape as early as 1970, when he directed a five-day national ecumenical retreat, which brought together about 100 English- and French-speaking people from across Canada. In attendance was a cross-section of clergy and laypeople from the major Christian denominations, including the moderator of the United Church, and bishops of the Anglican and Roman Catholic churches. To this gathering he tried to relate what he was discovering in his own community: that each person, no matter how wounded, has a great dignity and the capacity to enrich others. He spoke of his own growing awareness of the fact that Jesus's saving work was finally accomplished through his dying among common criminals, as an outcast of society. These passages of scripture have special meaning for him: "The very stone which the builders rejected has become the chief cornerstone; this was the Lord's doing, and it is marvelous to see!" (Mark 11:10) and "The weak things of this earth God has chosen to confound the wise" (1 Corinthians 1:27).

The communities of l'Arche are a proclamation that salvation comes through the innocent people, the wounded and rejected of the world.

4

Keeping It Afloat

"This is a magnificent ideal, but it is impossible to live." This was the conclusion of a journalist from a well-known French magazine after she had spent a morning at Trosly visiting the homes and workshops and talking with Jean Vanier about his vision of l'Arche. Vanier himself has spoken of it as a kind of foolishness: "This folly is the very basis of our community: to accept to live with people with developmental disabilities and in a certain way to identify with them, without renouncing our responsibilities." Is it livable or not? Let us look at the actual structure and organization, particularly that of the community at Trosly, to see how this vision took on flesh and bones and became a living reality.

If, in the beginning, l'Arche was simply a small, charismatic retinue, a group of friends led and inspired by Jean Vanier, there was nonetheless some sharing of responsibility and authority. Jean had some idea about what l'Arche might be, but he was also searching and eager to learn from the men he had welcomed and from the assistants. As mentioned, the first few months of living with Raphaël and Philippe did much to change and broaden Jean's idea of l'Arche. It would seem, and this naturally enough, that the first assistants who arrived did not immediately grasp and share his vision. But gradually, as more and more came to share in this vision, there was a growing sense that they were all joined together in a common adventure, in a new way of working with people with developmental disabilities, in a new type of Christian spiritual community without precedent or prototype. So, too, with Jean himself, the sense of adventure and the element of search had only become more acute with each new element that was introduced, whether it was the opening of a house in India or the creation of a workshop at Trosly.

The community structure gradually shifted from a charismatic retinue to a more professional type of organization (although Jean's inspirational leadership has remained important throughout the ongoing evolution of the structures). Such a shift implied an ever-greater sharing of everything from the vision and theory to the deployment of resources, the division of responsibility, the supervision and discipline. One key characteristic of this shift and the continuing evolution is the organic growth of the structure. Structure has not been conceived in an a priori manner and imposed from above, but has rather grown out of the concrete exigencies of the work and life of the community. For the most part, the structure has remained, even to this day, in the service of, and has not taken priority over, personal relations.

This organic growth was itself built into l'Arche, first of all in the form of annual meetings in which the entire structure could be reviewed and renovated in light of present needs and future expectations. In the early years this meeting was a weekend of discussions, reflection, prayer, and decision making that reviewed the previous year and planned for the coming year. This kind of annual meeting, to ensure a dynamically evolving structure, itself evolved with the increasing and changing dimensions of the community. Before long, it was split into two parts, with one weekend dedicated to studying the more temporal aspects of l'Arche, and another given to a more prayerful reflection on the spiritual needs of the community.

After some discussion, it was decided not to have the men and women with disabilities participate in the meeting dealing with the questions of organization, work, pedagogy, and so forth. Few of them would have been concerned with or able to grasp the significance of many of these issues. Also, some of the assistants felt it would be hard to talk freely of pedagogical issues in the presence of the core members. After 1969, then, this meeting was attended only by the assistants. All of them, even the most recent arrivals (60 persons in all), were invited to participate. The right to vote was restricted to those who had been at l'Arche for at least six months (54 persons).

This yearly meeting gave all the assistants, even those most recently arrived, the opportunity to participate in shaping the organization of the life and work of l'Arche. Such a structure helped to integrate new members quickly into the community, giving them a real share in the responsibility at a basic level and helping them to understand by a direct experience how the community was organized. What they could not help but sense here, as well as in the day-to-day living at l'Arche, was its provisional aspect. Its organization was not defined by a written constitution, as, for example, in most religious communities whose basic structure is established in a definitive way. In 1970, the first charter for the federation of l'Arche was written, and, as the federation rapidly developed, a first constitution was also approved. It has since gone through several major transformations. The organization of l'Arche was set up only one year at a time, thus giving it a great deal of flexibility. This flexibility and provisional nature reflected the aspect of adventure and search that is an important element of its spirit. With the opportunity to share quickly in the responsibility for the growth and direction of the community, the assistants were soon caught up into a sense of a common adventure.

Jean Vanier felt it was of great importance to try to maintain this twofold element of the provisional and flexible as l'Arche grew and its structure became more complex. Any growing organization naturally tends to become more structured and institutionalized, and l'Arche has not been exempt from this tendency. Even in the early '70s it was becoming an institution with little resemblance to the original gathering of a few friends around the person of Jean Vanier.

The government of l'Arche, Trosly and Cuise, was one of the major areas of discussion during the 1970 annual meeting, and it underwent considerable changes, as it had almost every year. That year the post of assistant director was created to help balance Jean's increasing absences and shoulder the growing administrative burdens. Certainly, part of the reason for creating this post was the presence of Antoinette Maurice, who was the obvious person to fill it. Other changes were effected so that the governance consisted of a director, assistant director, a major council, a council of those in positions of responsibility, and a general assembly. The major council consisted of the director and assistant director, three elected members, and two members named by the director (one of whom was Père Thomas). This council had the power to make major decisions, nominate to major positions or change those in major positions, accept or dismiss assistants, open new homes, and so forth. The second council was consultative and informative for the concerns of the major council and decision making for all current affairs. It included the director, the heads of the various homes, the director and assistant director of the workshops, the nurse, social worker, psychologist, secretary, and several other people responsible for different areas. The members of this council represented all the members of the community, and could make decisions concerning the normal functioning of the community. Each of these councils met once a week and when specially convoked to deal with specific issues. The general assembly was made up of all the assistants. It met every Monday morning to plan for the coming week, and to make certain more long-range plans.

This form of government was ordered toward giving a high degree of participation on all levels at which responsibility was exercised. The annual report drawn up by Vanier at that time noted, however, one evident lack in this participation that he hoped to see remedied in the coming years: having some of the core members elected to participate at some of these levels of responsibility. This hope was eventually realized. An obvious disadvantage in having such wide participation was that much time was given to meetings, thus taking the assistants away from their particular duties, and leaving them that much less time to be present to the men and women. This was not a serious difficulty, however, since the individuals with disabilities had the gift of calling the assistants to be present to them. (The more critical problem at l'Arche is that of assistants being able to be sufficiently present to and supportive among themselves. Periodically, ways have been considered to try to foster greater communion and mutual support among the assistants, a challenge that many struggle with and sometimes complain about.) The widespread participation in responsibility also gave rise to a certain overlapping and confusion of responsibility. As one man described it,

In a community like that, because everyone lives so closely together it's hard to know what position each person has, especially from the administrative point of view. I was often ordering supplies for work and it was interesting knowing who I was supposed to go to, or who I was to talk to to borrow stepladders and that sort of thing.

There's Mr.Vanier at the top and then there's three or four people under him, each one has a different duty but it isn't precisely defined. Then down below that you have people in the foyers [homes], and – well, I wouldn't want to say too much about it, but many times we did have difficulties as far as who really has the responsibility; perhaps better put, who can really accept the responsibility and be head of the foyer, and how do the duties work out. If one person has the responsibility of the foyer, what duties are expected of him?

I think this is what bothered me most because you weren't quite sure of your own position and what you were supposed to be doing when it wasn't clear from the top down.

Well, you wouldn't want it to be too professional, too clear cut. It's not a matter of one person giving orders to another person. You work together, but it does get confusing at times. I don't know whether this is Trosly or the French way of doing things, but I'd say things do get into a mess. It gets to be a joke after awhile. It all works out in the end.

This difficulty is mitigated by the climate of friendship and respectful personal contact in which are carried out the various exchanges of authority and responsibility. The frustration that is sometimes born of this confusion more often culminates in laughter or the exclamation "Alleluia!" than in an expression of anger.

There is also a certain structure, the general assembly, that allows for dialogue between the various levels of responsibility and so the possibility of working out some of these communication problems.

The general assembly, which met weekly for about an hour and a half, manifested both the element of widespread participation and the personal character of the government. This meeting was chaired by Jean Vanier, or in his absence by the assistant director, Antoinette. All the assistants who could make it to this meeting were gathered more or less in a circle, but quite informally, with no privileged positions.

Jean had the habit of showing a special warmth to those who had the humblest tasks in the community and who perhaps tended to be the most withdrawn. For example, when someone like the little elderly lady who helped with the housekeeping arrived, he welcomed her with a big smile and invited her to sit next to him. In the discussions that ensued, he was careful to elicit the opinions of those who were more quiet and shy. The whole tenor of this meeting was one of relaxed friendship, where there was much laughter and only rarely any tension or heated discussion.

Here there was an opportunity to freely express one's opinion or difficulties in the various aspects of the community's functioning. Fernand, who was in charge of the sports program, might have raised the issue of preparations for the forthcoming Special Olympics. Anne-Marie, the psychologist, might have spoken of a man who was just finishing his first two-week trial period at l'Arche, asking if this trial had indicated that l'Arche was good for him, and whether or not he should be brought back for a second trial of one or two months. Planning for a picnic or a day of spiritual renewal could be discussed: Michel giving his opinion insofar as it might involve closing the workshops early; others mentioning the need for transportation, the preparing of meals, the coordination between the various homes, and so forth.

So dialogue was established between people in various areas of responsibility: between the more permanent assistants and the newly arrived, between those who lived in the homes and those who came daily to work in the infirmary or the workshops or the laundry and the like, between those more concerned with the spiritual aspects of the community and those more concerned with the material aspects.

This general assembly contributed to the provisional and flexible aspects of the Trosly/Cuise community. Besides long-range planning, weekly planning and flexible adjustment to whatever unsuspected needs might arise also took place. Decisions made by the council could be communicated directly to all the assistants in this general assembly and, through them, to the entire community.

The provisional and flexible aspects also implied a certain fragility and vulnerability. It meant not only that the community could evolve, but also that it could disintegrate. Here we see a remarkable contrast with such professional organizations as hospitals, or such communities as the more traditional religious orders. Both of these types of organizations are highly structured, which protects them from adverse change, or any change whatsoever, for that matter. To consider only the aspect of the assimilation of new members offers a striking example. In a hospital, for instance, nursing students have no say in the organization during their years of formation; even as graduates they have little or no responsibility in shaping the organization. This, of course, is even more true for the orderlies, the maintenance staff, and so on, not to mention the patients themselves, who are basically reduced to passive objects. In contrast, the community at l'Arche has always been vulnerable to being changed by people who have had little time to be imbued with its spirit and meaning. This vulnerability was very real since, in fact, about half of those who had a vote in the 1970 yearly meeting had been at l'Arche for under two years.

This vulnerability or fragility, however, has a few obvious advantages. We have already noted that this approach integrates new members more quickly and totally into the community. Along with this integration comes the influx of new ideas and new life that these people bring to the community. The natural tendency of older members to become somewhat staid or self-satisfied is counteracted by the active participation of new members, who are continually arriving. The that's-the-way-we've-always-done-things attitude is constantly being challenged by those who do not know and perhaps do not particularly care how things have always been done. In the same way, the newly arrived women and men with developmental disabilities, because of the great freedom that is given to them, continue to challenge and call into question the "traditional" or "normal" ways of doing things.

An extremely important advantage of this fragile structure is the way it makes the entire community more responsive to the individual needs of the people with disabilities. Dr. Richet, the psychiatrist who assisted l'Arche in its early days, mentioned this fragility as one of l'Arche's most powerful means of helping the people who are welcomed. She contrasted it to the psychiatric hospital from which many of the men and women of l'Arche had come. The hospital, in its physical plant and its financial and governmental structure, was solid and unshakeable. This very solidity made it terribly unresponsive and insensitive to the needs of its "inmates." L'Arche, on the other hand, she noted, was an extremely fragile sort of thing: a group of typical, modest houses spread out in the village, with limited financial resources, with only a bare minimum of professionally trained staff, greatly dependent on volunteer help, capable of falling apart at any moment. But this very fragility made it much more sensitive to the individual members, and flexible enough to respond to the unique needs of each.

Finally, this fragility called for greater dependence on divine providence and a greater openness to the Spirit. Many spoke of a "spiritual force" keeping the community going, and of the spirit of trust in divine providence. Others added that their own trust in providence had been greatly increased as a result of being there. Some of this was attributed to Jean Vanier's own faith and to certain values predominant in the people with developmental disabilities, but also to "the lack of a strong organizational structure…the lack of material wealth," and "the openness to anyone who comes along" – in other words, to this element of fragility. The more people or communities can rely on their own strength, on their human capacities and material resources, the less they experience a need to rely on others. The very fragility of the core members disposed them in a unique and life-giving way to depend on others and on the Other. This quality or personality structure of feeling the need for help that is specific to these individuals is reflected in the structure and organization of the community as a whole.

Coupled with this aspect of fragility is that of the provisional and evolving. The community was on the move, but no one was sure where it was going. There was no prototype and few guidelines, so there was a deeply felt need to get guidance from somewhere. Needing guidance disposed the community toward a real openness to the Spirit. This aspect of the community's structure was perhaps more a reflection of a certain disposition of many of the assistants, who more consciously bear the responsibility for the growth and direction of the community. It is the assistants, also, who are more consciously concerned about the direction of their own lives. Many have given themselves totally to l'Arche. On the other hand, many of the assistants at l'Arche who, at least in their own hearts, have made some sort of commitment to the community remain in great uncertainty. Not only do they live with the incertitude that their own commitment is not definitively determined, but they are also aware that all the others with whom and to whom they are committed share a similar uncertainty. Furthermore, they live with the awareness that neither they nor anyone else quite knows where the community is going. This presents a kind of risk and uncertainty that can be extremely painful but that greatly disposes them to a constant recourse to the Spirit for guidance.

The various degrees of commitment and levels of participation of l'Arche's members also make of it what can best be described as an open community.

First, with regard to duration, we mentioned that many people come to l'Arche for only a limited time. This limit may or may not be fixed in advance. Patrick came for two days, and left seven months later. John was picked up by a carload of l'Arche people who were returning to Trosly after a weekend at Ambleteuse. He was hitchhiking from England to Spain at the time. With no fixed destination and no deadlines there was no reason not to stop in at Trosly. Four months later he was still there, with no plans to move on. Less frequently does it work the other way, where someone plans to stay for a year, but then leaves before the time is up. In any case, there is a constant flow of people. They come for a few weeks, a few months, a year or more. They share in the life and work of the community, giving of themselves, of their time and talents, receiving much in return and then finally moving on. Bonds of friendship are created that make departures very difficult. Even when departures are fraught with a sense of defeat or failure, these bonds often remain intact. The primary task of l'Arche is to help those who live there, first the individuals with developmental disabilities and then the assistants, to achieve the greatest possible human and spiritual progress. This task is in no way frustrated by such a continual flow of people coming and going – quite the contrary, because such a primary task is founded on an openness and mutual respect by which each can achieve the maximum liberty that is possible for him or her.

Regarding the degree of commitment, there is also great flexibility. At l'Arche it is not an all-or-nothing proposition. Some commit themselves only with regard to their professional services, coming from some distance to spend their eight hours a day at l'Arche and then returning to their home and family or to their bachelor apartment or wherever they may live. They may be a member of a religious congregation. One nun came to Trosly to run one of the workshops. She returned each evening to her little community of sisters in another village several miles away, and it was with that community that she shared her domestic life, leisure time, and life of worship. Even for such people l'Arche is usually not just another place to work, however. Their work there has a certain element of gratuitousness and self-gift. They may or may not share considerably in the life of faith and worship, but because the life calls forth this gift of self, they are very much a part of the community.

On the other hand, there have always been people who live and work quite apart from l'Arche, but who share to a great extent in the faith life and worship of the community. For example, a number of French college students often came to Trosly for the weekends or for a week or two at a time. To facilitate their coming and going, Père Thomas placed a little home, La Grange, at their disposal. La Grange was off to one corner of the village and was independent of the l'Arche administration. A little later, La Ferme, a complex of lodgings, library, and chapel clustered around a courtyard, was established to this same end. Besides the handful of local villagers who participated in the Sunday worship and other pastoral ministries of Père Thomas, others came to live permanently at Trosly, precisely to be able to share in the faith life and worship while otherwise living quite independently of l'Arche.

Many others became committed to l'Arche on a more full-time basis, with that sort of total gift that is characteristic of religious consecration. But even here a multiplicity of variations was in evidence. Many were unmarried, some having the intention of remaining so, for this was how they felt called to love and serve God in and through this community. Married couples, with or without families, have also been part of the community. From the outset, membership has included consecrated religious, such as Père Thomas himself, who was committed to remain at Trosly for the rest of his days while continuing a limited contact with his confreres and obedience to his superiors in the Dominican Order. Religious men and women participated totally in the l'Arche community for three or four months during the summer, or even for a year or more at a time, including, during the late '60s and early '70s, many North American Jesuits.

It should be noted that Père Thomas, who was so much at the heart of the community, lived apart from the other members. His home was one small room behind the sacristy. There he lived very simply, praying, preparing his sermons and talks, counseling a number of the men and women with disabilities, assistants, and others who came to see him. He did a considerable amount of visiting of the sick and those in the nearby psychiatric hospital, attended council meetings, but only rarely accepted invitations to take a meal or participate in other social events in the homes. But this withdrawal did not make him less present to the community. Quite the contrary: he was most present, being totally given to the community, in a clear and unambiguous way, as a man of the Spirit.

A few others also lived this more secluded type of existence at the heart of the community. These were people who participated fully in the work, direction, faith, and worship of the community but who had their little home or couple of rooms apart in the village, where they had the possibility of greater silence. These also were not less present to the community, but simply lived a more contemplative life within it.

Finally, a few assistants participated in almost everything except the faith life and worship. Most of them admitted to sometimes feeling a bit left out of things, but they were grateful for the freedom to live there under these conditions.

A further variation to this already wide range in levels of participation was the matter of financial remuneration. Some were paid a full salary from the moment of their arrival, while others who were full-time at l'Arche refused a salary altogether. The normal procedure, although there were some exceptions, was that those who came with professional skills were paid the current salary for such skills. Those who came without professional skills and acted more as volunteers wishing to share in an experience of community received a small amount of spending money if they committed themselves to stay for about a year. If, at the end of a year, they wished to commit themselves on a more permanent basis, and their presence and work were judged by the major council as adequate, they would be offered a regular salary. A few returned a part of this salary to the community out of a desire to live in a greater spirit of evangelical poverty.

The amount of salary received was never an indication, one way or another, of the degree of generosity and self-gift by which the individual might be committed to l'Arche. Some received a good salary and lived elsewhere than at Trosly, yet their dedication to the men and women and to the whole work of l'Arche was outstanding. Others, who were at Trosly on a volunteer basis, receiving no salary, sometimes manifested less of this quality of self-gift and presence. Nor was it always those who participated most fully in the life of worship who manifested the greatest generosity in giving of themselves.

In those early days a certain central core or inner circle of assistants assured an element of stability for the life and spirit of the community. This was not a juridical entity, although it included all those in the major council and many of those in the general council. At one point an effort was made to give a juridical structure to just such a central core by creating a group of "permanent assistants" who were personally committed to upholding the spirit defined by the statutes. They had the power to decide for or against accepting assistants on a permanent basis after their first year at l'Arche. They also were empowered to elect a new director after the retirement or death of Jean Vanier. For various reasons this organization of permanent assistants never proved satisfactory. For one thing, the statutes of the permanent assistants did not find their place within the larger organization. Soon a restructuring of the organization took away the permanent assistants' only authority by giving to the major council the authority to accept or dismiss assistants, and giving voting rights to all who had been at l'Arche for at least six months. It remained to be seen whether some new definition could be given to the permanent assistants. Most of this group participated fully in the faith life and worship of the community, with one or two exceptions. In fact, it comprised almost the whole gamut of variations of levels of participation that have just been outlined. In later years, some of the longings of assistants for a sense of meaning and commitment have been satisfied by announcing a "covenant" relationship with God and with their brothers and sisters in l'Arche.

But it is not only the assistants, or a core group of assistants, who assured a certain stability and spirit in the community. The core members themselves are very much responsible for the spirit of the community, and are finally the real guarantors of its stability. There is, in fact, a far greater turnover of assistants than of the men and women with disabilities who are the heart of l'Arche. Several of the men have been at Trosly since the founding of the Val Fleuri; that is to say, they have been there even longer than Jean Vanier (this continues to be true even in the year 2005). The people with disabilities maintain the spirit of the community with little conscious effort by their natural simplicity, openness, and capacity for affection. It would perhaps be more accurate to say that the assistants are there to animate these core members and call forth their gifts. The assistants have the responsibility to ensure that, with the growth and evolution that take place, the organization and structure of the community remain at the service of the person.

There is also among the people with disabilities considerable variety with regard to their level of participation in and commitment to the community. Besides the large number who live at Trosly, a sizeable group lives in family placements or foster homes, and some live at home with parents or other relatives. The latter two groups come to work at l'Arche and form something of a basic community among themselves and the assistants with whom they share the noon meal. A few of the men and women who live in have their work outside in factories, shops, or elsewhere, independently from l'Arche. Some of them have a strong sense that their stay at l'Arche is only a stage toward integration into "normal" society. Others feel that l'Arche is where they will live out the rest of their lives. Some are uncertain about this issue, and a few are perhaps not aware enough to consider the question. Some are capable of organizing most of their own leisure time, while others depend on the assistants to do so. Some participate fully in the faith life and worship, others only minimally, and some not at all. Some have good relationships with their families and spend every weekend and holiday with them, while others see their families rarely or not at all. For a few of the men and women, l'Arche is just another institution to which they have been committed – perhaps somewhat better than the last one they were in, but still an institution. A fair number do have a sense of the mission of l'Arche as a Christian community witnessing to the gospel by its spirit of unity, peace, and joy. A growing number consider the possibility of a personal call to commit themselves to live out their faith in Jesus in and through l'Arche.

L'Arche is also an open community, in that the external boundary allows for participation at many different levels or degrees. For one thing, this means that some members of the community will find their primary support relationships elsewhere, either in their families, their religious congregations, or with other friends, thus keeping the community inserted into the greater society in a vital way. It cannot easily become a ghetto or a sect. Such openness also allows for a good deal of personal freedom. No one forces individuals to commit themselves to more than they are ready for, or to assume certain responsibilities as part of a package deal, as in the Roman rite of the Catholic church, where a man has no choice but to be celibate if he wishes to be a priest, and a woman has no possibility for priestly ordination.

At l'Arche, the freedom to participate in the faith life and worship as one feels the need or the call encourages a personal and interior appropriation of the faith. No doubt some people would profit more from a situation that was more structured and that imposed certain religious practices by rule, but at least here there is a high degree of authenticity. People pray and worship not because of any exterior law, but because of some inner need or call.

Furthermore, with its wide variety of participants, l'Arche in some ways embodies all the different elements of the whole church. It is an example of the universal Christian community which, at its best, maintains an openness to people of other religious traditions as well as those without any religion. L'Arche is a community of laypeople, religious, and priests; married people, single people, and widows; those who have freely chosen to be celibate and those condemned to it by nature or circumstances; some whose vocation is more contemplative, and others more active, and some whose vocation is more charismatic; believers and nonbelievers, traditionalists and progressives, old and young, rich and poor. They are all together working for a common goal in a common spirit. Such a variety of people meeting one another precisely as people in all their uniqueness necessarily generates considerable creativity and life.

To this point, all that has been discussed about the organization and structure has been mainly with regard to the community at Trosly. It remains to say something about l'Arche taken in the widest sense to include the other communities in France and elsewhere.

In the early stage, the bonds between these various communities were primarily spiritual bonds – that is, of friendship and of the inspiration of Jean Vanier, and the concern to live out a common vision. At first, all the communities of France had the same overall board of directors, with Jean as the president. However, the director of each of the communities was given a great deal of freedom to run the community as he or she thought best. In one of the communities the director took an independent attitude to Trosly. Her approach was to treat the people she welcomed as patients to be cured, rather than simply as people with whom to share life. She was given the freedom to pursue this approach, but it proved unsuccessful, and eventually the board of directors had to move in to remedy the situation. This experience pointed out the risk of giving so much liberty to each individual director, but it did not provoke any immediate change in policy.

The one board of directors was the organization with ultimate responsibility for all the l'Arche communities in France. It was recognized by the government, and received through social security and social welfare the necessary funds for the daily running of these communities. Each center presented a yearly budget to be approved by the prefecture of the department of France in which it was located. (Eventually, the numerous communities of France would each have their own board of directors.) This system assured funding for the daily operating expenses, but it also imposed on the community the obligation of careful control of its spending. For expansion and the improvement of facilities or unexpected expenditures, money had to be acquired elsewhere, from private donations, loans, and so on. In those days, enough money was forthcoming to allow a fairly rapid expansion. Whatever money came in was quickly spent to purchase more property or make other improvements to accommodate the waiting list of people with disabilities who had no work and who often lived in inhuman conditions.

This financial structure did not impose on the members of l'Arche a life that could be called poor, but it did imply a modest kind of living. There was nothing fictitious about the spirit of poverty of those who constantly struggled to keep the food costs and other spending reasonably within the per diem cost allowed for by the budget. More important, this structure guaranteed that the community would not become a sect or closed little world, with minimal reference to the larger society. Whatever the spiritual aspirations or religious ambience of the community, it had to remain relevant to the larger community in which it was firmly rooted and to which it was always answerable.

Until 1972, the communities outside of France were totally independent from one another and from Trosly. Then, in 1972, the directors of all these communities met in Trosly and formed the Federation of l'Arche, a loose bond that left each member community free to develop according to its needs, allowing it to be more integral to its own society and culture.

Jean Vanier himself was the strongest link between all these communities. He was on hand in Bangalore when Asha Niketan (Home of Hope) opened its doors to its first members. He remained there with them for a month. For a number of years he would spend one month in India each year. Soon the groundwork was laid for the new Asha Niketan in Calcutta. On his twice-yearly trips to North America, he managed to spend some time at Daybreak (Richmond Hill, Ontario) and in the rapidly expanding number of communities that followed in Ottawa, Edmonton, Calgary, Winnipeg, and Erie, Pennsylvania. His role in these communities was not that of a superior or director but a friend, adviser, and inspirational guide.[8]

The unity of spirit is also due to the fact that, as it happened, in all the centers the director and/or some of the assistants had lived and worked for some time in the community of Trosly. This has created deep bonds of friendship among the assistants and also between assistants and the people with disabilities in different centers. The joy with which Agnes and Adriano from La Merci, for example, were welcomed at Trosly was an obvious indication of this deep friendship. The various communities in France also had frequent exchange visits of small groups, or even of the entire community, so that friendships between the people in different centers continued developing.

Since each community had considerable independence, each took on a unique character, although there was a certain spirit common to them all – the same spirit that animates Trosly. Valinos, a center for women, began with a woman at its head. La Merci began not as a home but simply as a sheltered workshop for men and women under the direction of a married couple; the wife was in charge while the husband finished a doctorate in philosophy. The Tremplin (more closely united to Trosly) was a kind of halfway house for men and women moving toward integration into society, and was run by a retired industrialist. Some of these individuals were eventually able to enter into marriages. Most of them worked in factories and shops in Compiègne. Daybreak was also founded by a married couple, with the husband in charge; it was the first center to have a director and quite a few members who were not Roman Catholic. The property was the gift of a congregation of religious sisters, Our Lady's Missionaries. These sisters and many other friends were Catholic, so the community took on a decidedly ecumenical spirit. Asha Niketan was the first center to be founded in a developing country. Although Gabrielle, the director, was not Indian, she made every effort to ensure that the community be an integral part of the society and culture of Bangalore. The board of directors were all Indian, and the spirit was ecumenical and interreligious, with Christians and Hindus praying together daily.

The exchanges between these communities was particularly enriching precisely because of this plurality. As the mother community continued to expand and evolve, it drew on the experience of these other centers, constantly appropriating and assimilating what it was receiving from them, and in turn nourishing them with something of its own life and character.

The very fragility of the bonds that link these various communities called forth a need and desire for an ever-deeper spiritual unity. One could sense this unity, for example, at Trosly, in the intensity with which prayers were said for the other communities (often mentioning by name the directors and other members) at the Eucharist and other prayer meetings and in the evening prayer in the individual homes. The Faith and Light International Pilgrimage for people with disabilities and their families and friends that took place at Lourdes on Easter 1971 was a rare opportunity for the various communities of l'Arche to come together and thus strengthen this unity. Most of the members of each community were present – some 200 people in all. (Asha Niketan was the only community not represented; its absence was felt deeply, and it was in some way made present in the spirit by the way members were thought of and prayed for by those who attended.) Besides meeting frequently during the pilgrimage itself, the communities spent a day together after it officially ended.

The whole tone of this special day symbolized something of what l'Arche is all about. There were no big discussions on policy or structure and organization. From the late afternoon when they gathered, until the next morning when they separated, the whole atmosphere was one of joyful celebration. They played, sang, danced, and prayed together in a joyful spirit of friendship and unity. Young men and women (and some not so young) from Canada met and were immediately at one with those of the various centers of France. The fact that the latter spoke only French posed few or no barriers to communication. They all spoke a common language, the language of the innocent, which most of us have long forgotten. As the groups parted to return to their own centers, the singing and dancing, the embraces and handshakes, the laughter and the tears clearly showed that the real force guaranteeing a continuing communion was the power of the Spirit at work in their hearts.

This power of the Spirit is ultimately the only explanation for the continuing survival and growth of l'Arche. However much has been said about its organization and structure, the structure, in fact, is much less visible than it may appear from this chapter. Women and men who have been there know that something beyond the structure keeps it all going. As one person remarked,

> It had already been going about five years when I went there. I was there for about a month or a month and a half before I realized that there is a spiritual force that must be keeping it together because it is so loosely organized.

Another spoke of it in a similar way:

> Sometimes you feel that the way the place is run, the way they are open to everybody and the amount of stuff that they put up with – this is absolute folly, what they are trying to do. Then you stand back after three months and you look and you say, "It works, for some reason or other." Also, there are a lot of tensions there and the whole show could just go up in smoke tomorrow, yet somehow or other it doesn't. It just keeps on going and fantastic things happen. It's just this unbelievable trust that impressed me -- a trust that God will work this thing out.

Certainly, some of the success is due to the genius and charism of Jean Vanier. As someone pointed out, "Vanier has the genius of keeping this unstructured thing going, and it works." Another noted,

> It's like today. All week long we had been planning to go to the sea today, and all week long it has rained. So today it's nice out. Everybody says it's a kind of Vanierism – you just hope for the best and it always works out.

However, it is obviously something more than Jean Vanier that keeps l'Arche going. The people who live there are convinced of this. One man puts it simply, and speaks for many there when he says, "It is something deeper than the influence of Mr. Vanier – I think it is the presence of Christ." This belief holds many at l'Arche and so makes it a living organism.

5

The Pain of It All

Almost everyone who comes to l'Arche is immediately impressed by the spirit of joy that prevails. Yet anyone who comes to know the community more intimately cannot but be impressed, even overwhelmed, by the amount of suffering that is a part of its daily life. The living out in great intensity of these seemingly opposite experiences, joy and suffering, might be called the particular grace or vocation of l'Arche. Both suffering and joy are an integral part of daily existence there, but both have their moments of greater intensity and more external expression. Instances of crises and death crystallize the suffering. Joy reaches its climax in moments of celebration. One, however, is never entirely without the other, especially because both find their ultimate meaning in birth, death, and resurrection – the single and total mystery of life.

Much has been said already concerning the suffering of men and women with developmental disabilities, which is essentially that of rejection, of being categorized as different and inferior. For those who would protest that such individuals are not conscious enough to recognize the looks of disdain, pity, or fear that are constantly being cast at them, we need only point out that even little babies, whose intellects have scarcely begun to function, know instinctively whether they are loved. Furthermore, children's continuing growth, even their very survival, depends on their receiving not only physical protection and nourishment, but also a certain amount of acceptance and human affection. It is true that, having lived this experience of rejection for some 20 years or more, the young adult with developmental disabilities usually has built up protective barriers that may lessen the intensity of this suffering; nonetheless, this history of rejection is borne constantly within, even after the person has spent several years living in a community such as l'Arche. Scars and open wounds remain that even a lifetime may not be sufficient to erase or heal completely. All of those welcomed at l'Arche have their own unique and poignant history of suffering; there is hardly any point to offering multiple examples. One incident, however, is perhaps worth recounting, for its very simplicity and because to some extent it shows that even moments of joy do not exclude or erase this suffering.

At the Special Olympics for people with developmental disabilities that took place in Paris in 1968, Jean-Charles, participating for the first time in any such competition, won a gold medal in the long jump. As he came down off the podium with the shining medal around his neck, tears streamed down his cheeks. His first words to Michelle, who had helped train him for the event and who was waiting to congratulate him, showed that his tears were not purely tears of joy: "Now will my parents believe that I'm worth something?" he said. In a real way, these men and women are for most of society like the Suffering Servant of Isaiah 53:2-3:

> He had no form or comeliness that we should look at him, and no beauty that we should desire him. He was despised and rejected by men; a man of sorrows, and acquainted with grief; and as one from whom men hide their faces he was despised, and we esteemed him not.

In addition to the experience of rejection, the other broad area of the suffering for people with developmental disabilities is that of being condemned to a life of radical dependence on others. Most of them will never be autonomous enough to marry and raise their own family. Their awareness of this reality is a source of great suffering. It is especially in this life of dependence that they experience their own human poverty. In this they can be understood as "the poor in spirit of the Gospel," who, because of their suffering and their dependence, are very much disposed to receive the Good News of salvation.

The amount of suffering experienced by the assistants at l'Arche is remarkable and not as easily accounted for. Of course they empathize with and profoundly share in the suffering of the core members, but this alone does not explain why so many are seemingly at the limit of their endurance in one way or another – physically exhausted or suffering interiorly or both. This does not mean that they drag themselves around with long faces – in fact, passing visitors see nothing but the joy of the community. No, their tears are usually reserved for moments when they are alone or with the chaplain or an intimate friend.

Their fatigue is easily understood. Besides the more practical work of administration, supervision of workshops, housekeeping, and the like, all the assistants participate in the all-important life of being present to the core members in a deeply personal and accepting way. People with developmental disabilities have a real thirst for intimacy, partly because of having been deprived for so long of healthy relationships, and partly because their limited intellectual capacities make them especially apt to live on the level of affections and of personal relationships. The difference between being at table with a group of so-called normal people and being at table with the folks at l'Arche is a good example. In the former case, we may have a stimulating, even taxing, conversation about some important political or social issue, or even about more personal aspects of our own lives, yet it usually remains little more than an exchange of ideas. On the other hand, at l'Arche, with Jean-Claude, François, and the others, there is little or no exchange of ideas. The content of our conversation is elementary. What is most important is that we are communicating. Their looks and their few words and gestures, or sometimes their profusion of words and gestures, are important because they are signs and questions of the degree to which they are accepted and loved for themselves. I am forced to be present and to give of myself much more out of the depth of my person in this latter situation. This kind of relationship can be fulfilling and joyful, but in the long run it can also be exhausting. Some of the assistants spend time with the men and women through much of their waking hours and so live constantly in this kind of intensely personal way. This explains why they are so tired, and why many discover a great need for periods of solitude to nourish and replenish themselves in the depths of their being.

Some assistants, after spending some time at l'Arche but before making any kind of permanent commitment to it, go through a painful period of indecision. They begin to discover that l'Arche is a world with values that are very different from – and in some ways opposed to – those of the world in which they used to live, and in which their families and many friends usually still live. They begin to wonder which of these two is the "true" world. Somehow they sense that giving themselves totally to the world of l'Arche could mean losing contact with that other world: the world of efficiency and competition, of fine clothes, restaurants, and other forms of distraction. Their frequent trips into Paris or other cities are at least in part a kind of testing to see if they can still be a part of that other world. The difficulty of re-integration for a person leaving l'Arche indicates that this problem is not purely imaginary.

These individuals have discovered something worthwhile at l'Arche, and feel an invitation or call to commit themselves more totally to l'Arche itself or at least to this kind of lifestyle. Some see it as a call to accept the Lord and the demands of the gospel. At the same time, they sense that such a commitment implies an important renunciation, a giving up of the very possibility of participating further with any kind of ease in the world symbolized by *gai Paris*.

A much deeper level of suffering is experienced by a few of those who have already made a more total commitment to l'Arche. This happens especially with people whose personality remains unstructured by professional training or other kinds of formation. This lack of structure means that they are extremely open and can relate to people with developmental disabilities simply and directly, person to person, without the limiting hierarchies of educator to student, or doctor to patient, or the like. But such a lack of structure also implies a defenselessness, a fragility. Because they are so open and defenseless, they can be easily wounded, much like the people with developmental disabilities. These assistants, though they may have few responsibilities in the community, are extremely important. They identify most completely with the men and women with developmental disabilities and do the most to create the unity between the two groups. They suffer because of their fragility and openness, and sometimes because they have little experience of their usefulness in the community. Often, through a life of prayer, their affectivity is gradually assumed into an interior growth – a growth that usually involves an increasing identification with the poverty and weakness of Jesus in the crib and on the cross, and the deepening acceptance of St. Paul's insight that our very weakness is our strength: "Because when I am weak, I am strong with the power of Christ" (2 Corinthians 12:10). Unfortunately, today there is less and less room for such fragile assistants as the communities become increasingly structured and accountable to government agencies.

In considering the organization and structure, we spoke of the insecurity in which some of the assistants are called to live. This is felt most deeply by those who are unmarried and still undecided as to whether to choose this single status as a way of life. Some, in fact, sense a real call to give themselves totally to l'Arche's work and life precisely in this state of celibacy. To respond to this call is not easy in a community where men and women live in such close relationship. Yet it is especially through such intimacy that a celibate life can in fact be lived creatively. Once such a choice is made, the insecurity is greatly relieved. However, it still remains a more difficult vocation than that of consecrated religious, who have declared publicly that they have made this choice. Those in the latter situation usually have the support of their community, of other women or men who have made this same commitment. The vocation to celibacy in a community such as l'Arche must be reaffirmed daily. It can be sustained only by an active faith in God and in this way of life.

This vocation to celibacy on the part of the assistants is very important. It is a source of strength and encouragement to the men and women who are condemned to celibacy by the fact that they cannot assume the responsibility of marriage. Often it is precisely when they realize that they cannot marry the person they love that people with developmental disabilities face most deeply their human limitations. For many of them, the ability to marry is the very touchstone of normalcy. Seeing others who could marry – but freely choose not to – opens to them the possibility of assuming their own celibacy as a vocation.

The married vocation at l'Arche is not without its own kind of difficulty. The life there calls for such consuming presence to all those in the homes and workshops that a married couple often feels torn. To be present and supportive to each other and to their children in this situation can be a source of much tension.

Finally, it should be noted that in some ways l'Arche tends to attract people who are fragile and who have already known considerable suffering. Such people find there the possibility of giving some meaning to their suffering. Certainly, a number of assistants also have disabilities in relationship to a competitive society that puts much emphasis on technology and efficiency. They have come to l'Arche precisely because it provides a viable alternative to a way of life that was unsatisfactory and, in some cases, even intolerable to them.

Few of the assistants, however, have come to l'Arche because they simply could not cope with "normal" society. They come for a whole variety of reasons, from the most altruistic to rather selfish motivations. They may not necessarily suffer greatly at l'Arche, but almost all, if they stay long enough, do come to a deeper sense of their own poverty. To be called on constantly to give of themselves in intimately personal relationships forces them to discover some of their own limitations. To be faced with someone who is anguished and to discover no way of responding is a humbling experience. To discover in someone who has been rejected by society as "handicapped" human qualities far richer than I myself possess is also a humbling experience. Such experiences are part of the daily life of l'Arche. Most assistants are sooner or later forced to realize that people with developmental disabilities are their equals. They are limited in some ways and gifted in others, as is each one of us.

To encounter these "poor ones" is to come to know our own poverty. Such an experience for a believing person serves to deepen our awareness of certain essential aspects of our faith. For those with little or no faith, the discovery of their own poverty can be an especially frightening experience. They sometimes try to suppress a total recognition of it, as perhaps we all do to some extent. If they accept their equality with people with developmental disabilities, their own poverty, this can be a first step toward accepting or discovering a living and loving God. There are not a great many formal religious conversions among the assistants who come to l'Arche. This may be partly due to the fact that no direct work of evangelization is done, but a spirit of great acceptance pervades. Also, in such a community of the poor, we realize with frightening forcefulness the extent to which living for God means dying to ourselves. However, almost all come to a greater awareness of their need for others, and are usually better disposed to encounter the Other.

L'Arche, then, is a community of the poor in the sense of the suffering and the poor in spirit who recognize their radical poverty as human beings and their need for one another and for God. Suffering and the awareness of our poverty are powerful forces for unity in the community. Perhaps this is most concretely manifested when there is a death in the community. I think, for example, of the death of Claude. Claude had been at Trosly only a short time, but long enough to be known by all. He died unexpectedly one night, suffocating during an epileptic seizure. It was the first death in the community. The days that followed, and especially the day of his funeral, were a time of intense peace and unity. The whole event was corporately experienced as a kind of mysterious visitation of the Divine. Similar experiences have taken place in most l'Arche communities. When Kannan, a young man who had been

there only a short time, accidentally drowned at Asha Niketan in
Bangalore, Gabrielle, the director, wrote to all at Trosly:

> We sense so deeply that all that took place this Monday of
> Pentecost is in some mysterious way the work of the Holy Spirit.
> How else to explain this profound unity among us, after the ten-
> sions and crises of recent weeks? To the degree that God makes
> us enter into the mystery of death – of his Death – there is a joy
> so limpid, a peace so profound that inundates us….

People with developmental disabilities are extremely sensitive
and open to the mystery of death, as has been demonstrated on
occasions of the deaths of friends and relatives. They often live such
moments with great compassion and a deep faith that death is the
beginning of a new life. This is surely due to their innocence and
heightened affectivity, but also to their own suffering. Suffering and
poverty are themselves a foretaste or the seeds of death. All of us
vaguely sense this in our own suffering and in the suffering of others we meet. Not only does death, in the ultimate sense, unite the
community, but so do all those minor deaths: the epileptic seizures,
the depressions, the tantrums, and the more constant anguish and
frustrations and fatigue that are so much a part of daily life.

This unity that has its source in suffering is mostly communicated at a nonverbal level. The core members often have not even
named for themselves much of their suffering. The assistants more
commonly do not find it helpful to verbalize either their own suffering or their compassion for others. A look or a clasped hand is
all that is needed to show that one understands and is united to
the other in his or her suffering, and is often all one can muster
by way of a cry for help from the depths of one's own anguished
heart. Words, even at their best, are poor vehicles of communication in this domain. I observed that many of the assistants, on first
coming to l'Arche at Trosly, especially the college students from
North America, were baffled and somewhat dismayed by the silence
of the more long-term assistants. It usually took months to begin
to enter more deeply into the suffering of the community and
into the nonverbal communion that is part of the spiritual unity

generated by this suffering. Suffering is, both for individuals and for the community as a whole, a call toward silence and interiority – toward prayer.

The prayer life at l'Arche finds its source especially in this suffering and poverty of spirit. There are certainly no rules or obligations about prayer or the use of the sacraments. These are structured into the life from within, from the vital need to find support and strength in one's weakness and suffering. Many there feel deeply that it is only thanks to the daily Mass and some moments of quiet in the chapel that they can get through the day. Prayer and sacraments are an existential obligation for many – not a question of rules or habit, but of survival.

The prayer life for both the core members and the assistants is strongly centered on the Eucharist, on a belief that they meet Jesus in a special way through the bread and wine consecrated by the priest. The concrete symbolism of the Eucharist that can be seen and touched and eaten is especially meaningful for people of simplicity who live very much on the level of affections, and for people who are too tired or anguished to do much thinking. Both the assistants and the core members are drawn to daily worship out of a sense of their own poverty and their need and hunger for God.

Certain signs indicate the reality of the faith that many of the people with disabilities have in the Eucharistic presence. The fact that so many participate when they are perfectly free not to is one sign. Furthermore, it can be seen in their faces at moments during the service, especially at the consecration and communion. Many at Trosly also go regularly to the adoration (a prayer service centered around the Eucharist) on Tuesday evenings. The atmosphere during this hour, in which praying decades of the rosary is preceded by a few prayerful words from the pastor and followed by moments of silence, is charged with a peace and concentration that make one sense the presence of the Spirit in a way that is all but tangible. Often the people will speak of Jesus's presence in the Eucharist in a way that shows how real this presence is to them. Sometimes their words have an originality that confirms they are not repeating someone else's words – like André explaining to Claude, who was preparing for his First Communion, what Jesus does for him in communion. "You know, Claude, Jesus calms your nerves." Père Thomas had discovered that the unique way of catechizing the people with developmental disabilities was in relationship to the Eucharist. Furthermore, at Trosly it was striking to see that even those who did not go to the services would come to see Père Thomas (and now Père Gilbert) in moments of difficulty, and ask him to pray at the Eucharist for their mother who was sick, or a relative who had died, or for whatever else troubled them.

Nowhere was the unity of the community more profoundly experienced than at the Eucharist. Here especially, the assistants could become aware that they were on a level of equality with the most limited core members, and the core members could realize their equality with the assistants. In fact, here the poorest and most suffering had a place of predilection. The sermons of Père Thomas often recalled Jesus's desire to receive the little ones because they are the model for a truly Christian posture: "Let the little children come to me, for of such is the kingdom of Heaven" (Matthew 19:14). Furthermore, in worshiping daily with these "poor in spirit," one could become gradually more conscious of the fact that Jesus's privileged audience was precisely the poor and suffering. He pointed out that the proof of his Messiahship is that "the blind see, the lame walk…and the poor have the gospel preached to them" (Luke 7:22). The intensity of the faith of many of the people with developmental disabilities, their eagerness to be close to Jesus in the Eucharist, cannot but impress anyone who goes regularly to the services. So here at worship the assistants become constantly more aware that, at the most profound level of their existence, in their relationship with God, they must strive to put on something of that innocence of these privileged ones.

Furthermore, this is true even in regard to understanding and assimilating the gospel message. Père Thomas always insisted that in his preaching he had the impression that it was the men and women with disabilities who profited the most from hearing the word of God. This was also the experience of those at Trosly who participated in the monthly Bible vigils or in the hour of sharing prayerfully over the text of the gospel for the Sunday Mass. The core members tend to respond directly to the gospel, grasping what is essential without getting caught up in distracting intellectual debate. Often in these sharing sessions the assistants were reduced to a kind of awed silence in hearing the core members speak out of the depths of their hearts of this Jesus who is so real and important to them and of their struggle to put his message into practice. Here was a verification of the words of Karl Rahner, that God reserves to himself the science of the heart. The Holy Spirit can and evidently does speak directly in the hearts of those who have little intellectual capacity, or in those who, in the words of St. John of the Cross, have "dispoiled" themselves of their reasoning and imagining powers to encounter the Lord in that direct intimacy of heart to heart. Many of the assistants come to realize, therefore, the implications of the fact that Jesus's privileged audience was the poor in spirit. They are the most likely to understand his message and so to better understand the gospel. Those of us who rely more on intellect can only beg God for this kind of simplicity of spirit.

The faith dimension of life at l'Arche is the source of a tremendously dynamic spirit in the community. People with disabilities may be seriously limited and wounded in their intelligence, nervous system, and psyche. They may be incapable of doing much effective work; they may not always manifest any progress in these domains; they may even seem to regress. However, at the deepest level of their existence they are called into intimacy with the Divine, where their human limitations no longer hinder progress, and, in fact, seem to favor it. On this level there is an experience of equality and uniqueness. Each is a child of God, with his or her unique relationship to the Lord, and his or her unique relationship to the others in the community. They all need one another to progress in the Spirit, to go forward with Jesus toward the One Jesus calls "Abba."

Furthermore, when the assistants discover their radical equality with those who are, in some ways, the rejects of our society, they have a kind of lived experience of the radical equality of all people. In discovering in the despised and rejected Jean-Charles, Claude, or Jacqueline a brother and a sister who has much to teach me on both the human and spiritual level, I realize implicitly that no one should be despised and rejected. In principle, at least, many people of faith believe in the Fatherhood and Motherhood of God and the equality before God of every human being. This truth comes alive for many at l'Arche with a certain forcefulness. If these rejected of our society are so obviously dear to the heart of God and are such equal partners in any relationship of friendship that I might establish with them, then everyone is dear to God and is at least potentially my friend, my brother, or my sister. There is a growing sense, however vague and unstated, among many at l'Arche that forming community with the women and men with developmental disabilities, with the "poor," does not stop with the boundaries of Trosly or the other l'Arche centers. These are surely focal points, but the community of the poor in which one may be privileged to share at l'Arche flows outward to embrace the whole of suffering humanity.

6

The Heart of the Matter

One of the most extraordinary aspects of the experience of l'Arche is the quality and depth of the interpersonal relationships. It is especially this experience of deep personal sharing that enables the men and women there to live with their considerable suffering. On the other hand, it is the facing and accepting of suffering that is probably the most significant dynamic working to generate this level of sharing.

I have learned much about human relations while living at l'Arche. Perhaps no one has taught me more about this than a man I shall call David, with whom I now have a profound friendship. For two summers in a row, David and I were together at La Merci during the vacation month of August. Part of David's anguish can be traced back to the anguish and confusion of his mother, which in turn can be traced to her husband, who died as a result of the cruelties he suffered during his internment as a Jew in a Nazi death camp. David had a deep sense of the sacred, and so he was attracted to the religious ceremonies and to me, the priest. Because of his ambivalent relationship with his mother he was unsure of who he was and confused about how to receive and express feelings of affection.

What is important here is that, as a result of his history and experience, David had developed some extraordinarily refined techniques for annoying people, all of which he turned on me, probably because he was attracted to me. One of his techniques was to ask the same simple questions over and over again all day long, day after day. Another was to approach you face-to-face and put his two hands around the back of your head. While saying how much he liked you he would begin jerking your head forward. Looking you straight in the eye he could see exactly how you were reacting to this treatment, and he could feel immediately to what extent you were resisting or tensing up as a result of it. These were only two of a whole array of behaviors by which David would desperately try to relate to others out of all his confusion and need for love, or by which he could at least give himself some reason why others did not love him.

The first summer I lived with David in the close confinement of the house La Merci I grew to like him, but had no idea how to handle him. Usually, I would let him go so far with his annoying tactics until I felt I had to resist him. I would do this forcibly but with every effort to use no more force than was necessary, always trying to let him know that I still liked him. And so the month went by, with both of us growing a little in our liking for one another, but with little real change in either one of us.

The second summer arrived and David took up right where he had left off eleven months earlier. I, too, began just where I had left off with him, but perhaps a bit exasperated to realize there was going to be another whole month of David's ceaseless annoyances to put up with. Slowly I began to see that when I resisted him with force, the force was not totally under my control as an expression of my desire to help him. The force always controlled me to some extent, and became a subtle means of inflicting some revenge on my aggressor. A conversation with Jean Vanier at that time made me think and pray about my relationship to David. Jean pointed out precisely that one role of an assistant was to be a peaceful or nonviolent presence, to absorb some of the anguish of the core members that a life of rejection had engendered in them. I saw that any resistance to David was a kind of violence that only added another link to the whole chain of violence, in which he was a victim. So I adopted an attitude of greater receptivity and non-violent resistance, allowing him to do as he pleased with me.

I realize in retrospect that it was David himself, by his own acceptance and forgiveness of my aggression toward him, who greatly helped me to adopt this attitude. The first thing I discovered once I stopped resisting him was that a great deal of tension went out of me. I could now adopt a simple and consistent openness to him. The words I spoke were the same ones I had always used, but they had a much fuller meaning. I was not being dishonest earlier when I told him that I liked him, but to the degree that I resisted him I was failing to accept him as he was, and was preferring my need for peace and quiet to his need for love and understanding. I soon found myself no longer avoiding his company but rather seeking him out just for the pleasure of being with him. Although nothing seemed to have changed in his attitude toward me, something had changed considerably in me. This gift or grace came through David himself and through the community that encourages and supports such an attitude. There were, of course, still failures in my attitude toward him, but at least I began to experience a more unconditional love for him and, as usual, David was always quick to forgive me. Now it mattered much less to me that David change. I wanted him to grow, but my love for him was not given on condition that he grow and be different than he was. I could accept him more just as he was. In the lowering of some of my own barriers of aggression and self-preservation, the two of us came much closer together. With this greater closeness I could see a lot more of the goodness and beauty of his person, which one could scarcely fail to love.

It neither surprised nor disappointed me that there was no immediate change in David's conduct. What did surprise me was that after a couple of weeks he went into a quiet, reflective mood, during which time he ceased all his annoying habits. In fact, he simply avoided people. This lasted a few days, but even when he began coming out of this mood and being more himself, a striking change could be seen in him. His annoying tactics were greatly reduced, and he seemed to have made a real step forward in being able to relate to people more simply and directly. It is not my intention here to analyze what took place in David's experience. It could well be that his change in attitude was brought on by factors other than that of his relationship to me. We have each done much to heal and to free one another, but the issue at hand is primarily the change that took place in me.

This friendship has taught me something about myself and my limitations in accepting others. In helping me to lower some of the barriers that separated us, David has led me to a greater awareness of the ways I keep others at a distance and refuse to allow them to be themselves. Allowing him to be more himself enabled me to be more myself. It is clear that the acceptance of others is a direct function of the acceptance of oneself. This acceptance becomes increasingly more difficult in a community that seeks unity through some sort of conformity or uniformity rather than through the complementarity of the uniqueness of each of its members. The tremendously rich potential in friendships, marriages, parental relationships, religious communities, teacher-student relations, and many other human relationships is often never brought to any kind of fulfillment precisely because of this desire to make the other conform rather than to allow the other to be in all his or her uniqueness.

Our natural drive for self-preservation leads us to construct an array of barriers to protect us from others. Some of these barriers are necessary for survival, but barriers not only keep outsiders from getting in, they also keep insiders from getting out. So, the barriers we construct become in some ways our own prisons or coffins. The reasons for constructing these barriers are of course multiple and complex, but certainly a great deal has to do with our fear of being wounded or rejected – of being diminished or even destroyed. Latent in most of these fears is the fear of death itself. This understanding helps to explain why there is so much fear and rejection of such innocent and harmless people as Denis and David and others who have been deeply wounded physically, psychically, or socially. These individuals bear in an obvious way the signs of death. So, the natural tendency is to treat them as nonpersons. They are not persons to know and love but patients to be placed in institutions, or cases to be resolved by social legislation. My fear of the down-and-outer who asks me for money is not primarily a financial issue. Often, even in conceding to his request, I dare not look into his eyes, but simply look away or look through him with a kind of stare that says, "I want nothing to do with this thing, but just want to get it out of my way as quickly as possible." I cannot allow him to be a person, because a person is what I am. If he is a person, then in some way we are equal and he mirrors to me something of myself. He is a "dying" man and so my fear of death prevents me from seeing him as a man at all, for fear of seeing in him my own death.

Our freedom to be ourselves depends on our freedom to accept others, because it is only in relationship to other persons that the human person can blossom. In many ways, the greatest freedom comes in accepting the seemingly most unacceptable, those who most evidently manifest the signs of death.

This kind of freedom is not easily achieved in a technological society, where the value of interpersonal relationships is often lost in the shadow of the supreme value of efficiency imposed by the laws of economics and competition. Production then seems to become an end in itself rather than a means to human fulfillment, and individuals are valued only in terms of their capacity to produce. In a society with these criteria, people with developmental disabilities have no place. They must be rejected as useless. Production is also important at l'Arche, but it does not become an end in itself. Here even the work becomes the means by which personal relationships are enhanced.

I quickly grasped this latter truth in a visit to the office of l'Arche, Trosly, which seemed more like a coffeehouse than an office. The moment I met Barbara, Jean Vanier's "secretary" (the term is inadequate, since she fills a multiplicity of roles and seems to embody the very spirit of l'Arche), it was obvious that I was a long way from a corporate-type enterprise. Barbara's attire may have reflected the disorder of the office itself, but her joy and personal warmth distracted people from paying much attention to the surroundings.

The office is faithful to what it is called: *l'accueil*, which means the place of welcome. When I was tired and in need of a lift, it was usually to the office that I would gravitate. A great number of people passed through it each day. Besides administrators from other centers, businessmen, parents, heads of workshops and homes, and other visitors, many of the core members would come for visits. They came to meet the visitors, or to unburden themselves of some particular anguish, or simply to laugh with Barbara and the others who shared the administrative load with her. The phone rang constantly, and when the person who answered let out an "Alleluia!" it was a sure sign that the call was from one of the other l'Arche centers in France, or from elsewhere in the world. This type of call usually precipitated an explosion of joy, and many others – not just Jean Vanier or whoever was on duty – would come to the phone to exchange a few loving words.

Making oneself at home in the office usually meant clearing a space. Mounds of letters and other papers were piled on desks and chairs with photos, books on poetry or mysticism, cakes and cheese and perhaps a half-full bottle of wine or cognac. Vanier often encouraged Barbara to put some order into the place, but attempts at organization brought only limited results for the briefest periods of time. In spite of all the chaos, the business of organizing meetings, writing letters, and translating Jean's articles and books from French to English or from English to French somehow got done. This was largely due to the fact that in the quiet of the small hours of the morning Barbara was still happily at work.

One might best understand the significance of work for the women and men with disabilities by attending one of the meetings when they got together with the assistants to discuss the work. Held on the last Friday of each month, these meetings involved all the people from the workshops, gardens, and other areas of work. Michel, who was in charge of all the work, chaired the meetings. The Friday I am about to describe was a fairly typical one. It was scheduled to begin at 4:45. By 4:30 the room was already half full and charged with an atmosphere of friendship and joy like that of a group of young people preparing for a rock festival. By 4:45 the room was packed with about 80 people, including about 15 assistants.

Michel was sitting toward the front at one end of the semi-circle of people crowded together on chairs or on the floor. The room became somewhat quieter as he began to speak. The atmosphere of joyful seriousness and of great respect shown by Michel and everyone else toward whatever anyone had to say is not easy to describe. However, perhaps some of this will come through in the parts of the meeting that I will now present in a rough translation.

Michel [M]: Well, let's see. This makes how many times we have gotten together?

Several People: [shouting out spontaneously] Two! Five! Many! Eight!

M: Let's just see, now. We began in October. That makes [he counts them out on his fingers, and several of the guys say the months with him] October, November, December, January, and now February. So this is our fifth meeting. OK?

Several People: Yes! OK, Michel! OK!

M: And who can tell us why it is we have these meetings?

Jean-Paul: To consider the problems of the workshops.

Michel F.: To see what is being done in the different workshops.

André: [bursting with the desire to speak but not knowing what to say] Uh…for the work. Uh…to discuss things. Uh…

Claude: To talk about our work.

M: Good. So let's begin by seeing how things are going in the different areas of work. Let's start with the mosaics. Can someone from the mosaics give us a report?

Benoit: [raising his hand and shouting] Me!

M: OK, Benoit, go ahead.

Benoit: [in a rapid mechanical tone, and stopping as abruptly as he began] I'm making a clown!

M: Thank you, Benoit. Now what else is being done in the mosaics? Jean-Paul, can you carry on?

Jean-Paul: [with evident pride] Well, Benoit is making a clown, but we are doing all kinds of different designs: clowns, birds, the Blessed Virgin, and other things. And different kinds of things: for hanging on the walls, or putting on the table under serving dishes, tables…. We just sold a big table – one of those that George and Marcel made in the iron-works shop. Things are going really well. There is just one problem. Michel T. plays his transistor [radio] too loud.

M: Good. Now, we've already spoken about this business of the transistors. OK, Michel?

Michel T.: [scratching his head, and pushing up his glasses, he tries to smile, and mumbles a reply] Yes, OK.

M: Is there anyone who does not want any transistors in the workshops? Is there anyone who finds this annoying?

Several People: No! No problem! No!

M: Fine. Obviously no one should play his transistor so loud that it bothers people. Is everyone agreed about this?

Several People: OK! Agreed! Yes!

The two men who reported on the mosaics seemed to be such different people that it was hard to imagine them working together in the same shop. They were both blond and fairly tall, but here the resemblance ceased. Benoit seemed to be off in his own world, with little sense of the people around him. Jean-Paul showed few or no signs of having a disability. He had an extraordinary presence. He was very well groomed and expressed himself correctly. Evidently, however, making mosaics responded to a certain need or desire in both these young men. They were both happy to be there.

In this particular workshop, each person worked on his own, which made it possible for people of very different capacities to work there. Perhaps this was the outstanding feature of this workshop – a spirit of quiet concentration. Most of the eight or nine working there would look up and give you a smile as you came through the door, but then at least half of them would return to cutting and gluing the pieces of ceramic that made up the mosaic.

Jean-Michel would almost certainly come over to greet you, rolling up his sleeve as he came. He would welcome you with overly gracious words, then take your hand and place it on his bare forearm and hold it there firmly. If you were a stranger he would ask you if this bothered you, and, in any case, he would keep up a flow of conversation in order to hold onto your hand as long as possible. Meanwhile you might get him to show you his work. Usually it was a large and complicated design, which he executed with extraordinary finesse. He was evidently proud of his work, even though he found every possible excuse to avoid doing it.

When you got your hand back from Jean-Michel you might have offered it to Tiery, who worked next to him. Tiery occasionally responded with a brief and feeble handshake but more commonly just looked at your hand and then turned away. Only gradually would he look at you with a furtive glance, and maybe finally a smile or a laugh, but whether this was in friendship or mockery was not clear. Tiery had great difficulty concentrating on his work. He would hold a piece of ceramic in his hand for maybe ten minutes, looking at it, looking around the room, perhaps smiling to himself before he finally glued it somewhat carelessly to the simple little mosaic that he might have been working on for a month or more.

Philippe, next to Tiery, would be overjoyed to greet you and to show you with great pride the work he was doing. He might quickly turn the conversation to the film he had seen last night on TV, or to his slide collection and a request that you help him procure some slides from your part of the country or the world. Philippe expressed himself articulately but with his own unique logic that was not always easy to follow.

Claude and Michel T., who worked side by side, were evidently close friends. They spent much time conversing but without ceasing to work. Claude produced work of excellent quality. From time to time he would push back his chair, take his harmonica and play a few tunes that expressed his own peace and joy. Michel's work was hampered by his poor eyesight, but he was happy to be doing this artistic type of work and was proud of his accomplishments.

In the corner but facing toward the center of the room was Abdullah. Unable to speak, he would welcome you with a warm smile. He might begin to extend his left hand to you, but then, with a smile and a bit of an effort, offer you his slightly crippled right hand. Since beginning to do some physical therapy one afternoon a week, Abdullah was making more of an effort to use his right side. He would nod and grunt yes or no in response to your questions, but most of all he would simply smile and let you know by this that he was pleased to have you watch him work – something he did slowly and awkwardly but with very fine results.

The two or three assistants who worked in this shop would also greet you warmly, but then continue their work of designing or tracing out the patterns to be made, or looking after the accounts, or seeing to the minimum of supervision that was necessary. They were content to leave the business of public relations to Jean-Paul or Jean-Michel, who were more than happy to welcome visitors and show them around.

The atmosphere in this shop was usually one of quiet order, except for the moments that Tiery took it in his head to pour glue onto Lucy's hair, and, with a mischievous glint in his eye, chase her around the room until someone rescued her. The peace was also occasionally disturbed by a violent outburst when the usually gentle Abdullah lost his temper at someone, which was more an expression of his frustration at not being able to talk than something he really had against the person concerned. However, what was most impressive about this and most of the other workshops was the way the people accepted one another, the prevailing spirit of joy, and their manner of making visitors feel welcome.

Having received the report from the mosaics and having settled the difficulty about the use of transistors, Michel went on to ask for reports from the other workshops.

M: Well, let's hear from the workshop that is doing the lamps [assembling and packing them for a nearby plastic factory]. Can someone tell us how things are going here?

Michel F.: It's going great. We did a lot more this week than last.

Alain [the assistant in charge of all the work done for the factories]: I was at the factory yesterday. They are very pleased with our work, and have promised to give us a great deal more to do. In a month's time we will be handling between 60 and 70 percent of all their production.

M: That's great. Did you all understand what Alain just said? [He explains this in uncomplicated terms.]

M: Now the *bouchons* [the workshop that assembles the plastic bushings for the same factory]. Yes, Jenny's workshop. [Jenny is a young Canadian who supervises, or, rather, works along with the men in this workshop.]

Pierre: We are now working on an assembly line. It seems to be going well but I'd like to know how many we did this week.

Alain: I can't give you the figures yet, but Monday morning I'll let each workshop know what its production was for this week. OK?

M: And the others, how is the work going?

André: [again, bursting with a desire to speak but not knowing what to say] Uh . . . yes. It's going OK.

Patrick: [with a huge smile] I'm working hard!

M: And you, Jean-Charles?

Jean-Charles: [who mumbles] Yeah . . . OK.

M: Let's admit that you are not very often on the job, Jean-Charles.

Jean-Charles: [protesting but with no sign of embarrassment] Ah, no!

M: The work is going so well for our friend Jean-Charles that he spends most of the day walking around the village to tell everybody about it.

[Everyone bursts into laughter, including Jean-Charles himself.]

M: And how are things going in the *Sac en papier* [folders for storing archives or filing letters and notes]? Robert, you just arrived last week?

Robert: [nodding but seeming to be too shy to speak]

Jacques: [standing and assuming a businesslike attitude] We really turned in a day's work today, we made 350. It started a bit slow this morning. The fellows on the forms [the first operation in this small assembly line] were not on the ball this morning, but they sure turned it on this afternoon, and more than made up for it.

M: Yes, we'll have to admit that the fellows on the forms really worked, eh, Patrick, eh, George? [Patrick and George are all smiles.]

Finally they go on to consider how the work is going in the gardens, on the maintenance crew, and for those who help out in the kitchens of the different houses. Then Michel introduces another matter.

M: That's fine. Now we want to discuss the important question of salaries. We have already discussed before why the pay for each month is delayed. [They all receive a small pay each Friday, plus a larger sum once a month.] You know that all the money that comes in from the sale of mosaics, the folders, ironwork, and from the work that you do for the factories all comes back to you in salaries. Now the factories don't pay us right away for our work. The way they run their accounts, they can't pay us right away, but only about six weeks later. So it will only be next Monday, the 20th, that you will receive your monthly pay, and it is for the work you did during the month of December. Do you all understand this? [Many nod their assent.] Fine, so who can repeat what I just said?

Roland: Yes! Me! [he wants so much to be able to say something but has obviously not understood much of what has been said] Uh . . . Uh . . . Uh . . .

Michel F.: [taking over for Roland] You said that the factories are six weeks behind in paying for our work…uh…and that we will get paid on Monday.

Pierre: I've another question. What about this business of half of our salaries being taken away from us?

M: Good. I've explained this before but it's good that you bring it up again. That's right, half of each person's salary goes in to help pay for food, lodging, and the like. You see, a good deal of money is spent for these things, and it seems right, doesn't it, that you should help share these costs? This is important, so I hope everyone understands this.

Several People: Yes. Yes, Michel. OK.

George: [a big fellow in blue coveralls who is standing at the back just inside the door] No, I don't agree.

M: What is it you don't agree with, George?

George: I don't agree that half our pay should be taken and given to those who don't work.

M: But, George, you haven't understood Pierre's question. That's not the issue. Pierre, can you explain this to George?

After a few exchanges George seemed to be reassured. Part of his difficulty was a newly inaugurated system of grading people with disabilities into four categories according to their capacities to work. Michel explained that he would be happy to discuss one-on-one any difficulties that people might have with their own salaries. He stressed the fact that this was a private affair that he did not want to discuss in a public meeting like this. At this point Jacques raised his hand and asked just such a question: Why was it that he received only four and a half francs this week, instead of the usual five? Michel explained once more that such questions should be handled privately. Jacques continued to insist, until he finally understood that he would have to see Michel later in his office. Several other issues were discussed, and finally, when there were no more questions, the meeting was adjourned. Instantly, Jean-Claude, as was his custom, jumped to his feet singing Alleluia. A few others joined in the singing, or burst into noisy bantering and laughter, while others clustered in small groups to rehash what had been said during the previous hour and a quarter. The meeting ended as happily as it began.

The spirit that pervaded such meetings, as well as that which reigned in the workshops and other areas of work, showed something of the importance of work in the lives of these men. Michel and others who were responsible for this aspect of the life at Trosly could verify this state of affairs. The satisfaction of being able to work is in itself of tremendous value for people who, before coming to l'Arche, had never been able to have a steady job. You could sense immediately upon entering any one of the workshops that these individuals were not working just because they needed money, or because they were being forced to work. It was, for almost all of them, a joy to be able to work. One of the things they often mentioned in saying why they were happy to be at l'Arche was precisely the fact that here they could work. This would explain, too, why Patrick could say to me, as he did one Saturday, that he would be happy when the weekend was over and he could go back to work.

None of this is to deny that some, from time to time, have to be cajoled into going to work. Others cannot stay at their job unless an assistant stays beside them constantly to encourage them. On the other hand, some do not want to stop working and have to be told to stop – like Joseph, who worked in the gardens and especially liked cleaning up the flowerbeds, rose bushes, and the like. In his case, the only problem was that, if one did not pay close attention to him, when Joseph was finished the flowers and rose bushes were also finished, and nothing was left but the good clean earth. Another example is Daniel, who belonged to the maintenance crew. One day while working on a newly purchased house, Daniel finished the job he was given of scraping the old plaster off the walls. What next? He had to keep working, but there was no one to tell him what to do. He had heard that l'Arche had bought the adjacent property, which was separated by a brick wall. When Ken arrived two hours later, Daniel was just taking the last swing with his pick at what used to be a brick wall, in order that not a stone be left upon a stone. It was aesthetically and practically a fine thing to have joined the two properties. The only problem was that the adjacent property had not been purchased yet.

In spite of the occasional error, such as this one that left Daniel very disheartened for two days, working gives the core members a sense of their own worth. The salary they receive is important, not just because they need or want to have money, but also because it gives a value to their work. One time four or five of the guys went on strike to protest for higher wages. The main reason for their protest was not simply that they wanted more money to buy things, but rather a feeling that the work they were doing was worth more than they were receiving for it. Such a protest was a sign that they were achieving a certain freedom and independence and a greater sense of the value of their work.

There is, then, a way of speaking of progress with regard to the work: it is a progress in the individuals themselves, a gaining of a sense of self-worth in being able to produce, to do something worthy of praise, and deserving of a salary. Also, it is important for them to have money that they have earned themselves. Lucien bought himself a tape recorder; he had been saving money for it for over a year. His sense of achievement in having managed to save that much money and make the purchase on his own seemed to give him far more pleasure than the tape recorder itself. It means much to people who have been forced to live in such total dependence on others to be able to buy their own cigarettes or pay their own way. Some would buy cookies and candies primarily to have something to offer to others. Others, like René, who loved to smoke and who earned only enough to buy a couple of packs of cigarettes a week, would nevertheless be quick to offer cigarettes to his companions at work or at home.

With regard to their abilities and capacities to work, the term "progress" has much less significance. The occasional person, such as Michel P., does make remarkable progress; he seemed to be very limited when he arrived at l'Arche, but soon began to find himself in the workshops. In a little over a year he was working in a factory while still living at Trosly, and by the end of another year he had left l'Arche altogether to live a fairly independent existence. However, for the majority, no such progress is realized. In fact, for some people who have been at l'Arche almost from the beginning, there is often a certain regression in their productive capacity. L'Arche is not a school or a training center, but a community where people can, if they wish, live out their entire lives. There will be those who do stay and live through the period of decline that comes with age or with psychological regression.

In terms of the work at l'Arche, an element of stagnation is inevitable. Some people feel it acutely at times, especially those who have only mild disabilities and are more aware of their situation. Here a man who has been at Trosly for over five years comes to mind. Let us call him Charles. Charles has been in the same workshop for four years. Now 27 years old, he realizes that it is unlikely that he will ever be capable of assuming more challenging work than this. He will probably never be capable of assuming the responsibilities of marriage or even a more independent life. He is struggling to accept this reality, but finds it very painful. At times he is submerged in a state of anguish and depression. In some ways, this situation is not unique. Almost every adult sooner or later passes through the crisis of realizing that a certain limit has been reached with regard to their capacities or productivity and creativity. How many people in the corporate world, for example, at the age of about 40 come to the painful realization that they have nothing more to look forward to but the moment of retirement? However, the crisis can be particularly difficult for those whose productive and creative capacities are especially limited.

The assistants at l'Arche, depending on the degree of their sensitivity and capacity for empathy, suffer to a greater or lesser degree through such crises and more permanent states of anguish with the core members. The anguish of Charles, for example, becomes the anguish also of those assistants who are close to him. In some ways this is the essential work of the assistants: to be present to assume or absorb some of the anguish of those who are suffering from wounded intellects and nervous systems, and from the life of rejection that these wounds have incited. This aspect of the work of the assistants entails considerable suffering and unites them to those with disabilities in a unique way – by compassion.

This word "compassion" here must be taken in its literal sense: to suffer with. It is not a question of pity, but of entering into the other, of trying to resonate with the other. Sometimes the person in question may not be able to speak, or may speak with a logic that is unique to him, a kind of symbolic language by which he struggles to express something of his inner self, his suffering, his love, his meaning. The role of the assistant is to be present to such individuals, with a deep respect for who they are as persons, a respect they have every right to but may never have received. It demands on the part of the assistant a real sense of the dignity of the human person and sufficient interiority – as Vanier once put it, to "hear the music of the other," to appreciate the other in all his or her uniqueness, and try to understand and love them precisely in and for this uniqueness.

Certainly, there are more pragmatic aspects of the work of the assistants: cooking, housekeeping, running the workshops, nursing, administration, and so forth. For some assistants this more pragmatic aspect may be predominant, and may be the essential way in which they achieve a sense of self-worth. Those who do not find their place on this level are usually somewhat lost and suffer from a feeling of uselessness. Nevertheless, the primary work at l'Arche for all the assistants is to help the core members by creating with them a community of mutual respect and genuine friendship. There are assistants who do not share in the domestic life and leisure, nor in the worship of l'Arche, or perhaps in only one or another of these aspects: they work their eight hours a day, five days a week, but spend the rest of their time with their families either in the village or elsewhere. But even these people would scarcely be able to continue working at l'Arche if there were not something more than their salaries attracting them. For example, the nurse must do more than simply hand out pills. She must also communicate a certain element of gratuity, a gift of self that goes beyond whatever particular professional services or talents she might have to offer. It is almost impossible to avoid a certain gift of self because the people with disabilities, who live so much on the level of affectivity, call forth this gift from those who live with them. To be called upon constantly to give of oneself might at times be nearly unbearable, but it would be even more unbearable to try to live at l'Arche while refusing to give something of oneself. This issue of gift of self and of compassion touches the very heart of l'Arche.

Jean Vanier in Trosly, with Mira after the community Mass.

Gentle Woman statue outside the community chapel.

L'Arche Trosly – the original home where it all began.

La Ferme (the Farm) of l'Arche, a center of prayer and welcome.

Raphaël, Bill Clarke, and Lucien share a joke at the dinner table.

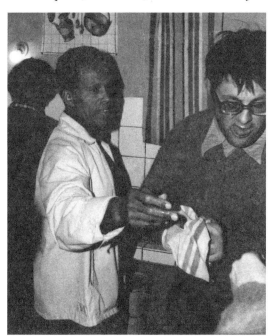

Everyone helps with the dishes.

Jean Vanier, Mother Teresa of Calcutta, and Père Thomas Philippe.

Madame Pauline Vanier, Jean's mother, in discussion with Père Thomas.

7

Enough Room for Joy

Along with the suffering that is so much a part of daily life at l'Arche is an overall spirit of joy that, to some extent, is born of that suffering. Although the joy is, in its profoundest forms, a pervading spirit in the community, it is especially expressed and nourished by moments of celebration. As Jean Vanier noted in a talk he gave to the community,

> But in addition to the daily life there is also the celebration – this is, as it were, the summit of community life. This is found already after a fashion, in the meals, the songs, and the encounters at the Eucharist. But there are times in the year when it is more intense: Christmas, Easter, birthdays, departures and arrivals, visits, Sundays, vacations, weekends, pilgrimages – celebrations which are not compensations for daily tedium, but which are like the flower which blossoms on the stem of everyday life.

He describes the effects of celebration on the individuals and the community as a whole:

> The celebration is that which relaxes people in the depths of their sensibilities, that which opens them to others and to the universe. It softens hardness of heart and spirit. It creates unity between persons. It is the sign of the happiness of the eternal celebration.

It is hardly possible to take each of these many instances of celebration and show that they indeed have the effects Vanier suggests, but it will be helpful to look at some of them more closely.

In general, this life of celebration has two centers of focus: the home and the chapel. Let us first consider the former. In the same talk just cited, Jean goes on to emphasize the importance of the home:

> These celebrations, just as the community spirit, imply a whole world of symbols, a "liturgy" of life. It is up to the whole of the community to live these symbols, and to the home to develop their own style of life – each one a little different from the others – and to create a feeling of belonging to the community. Thus it is good that each home develop its "liturgy" of meals, prayer in common, get-togethers, etc.

In fact, each home at l'Arche has its own unique spirit, but one discovers in each of them an underlying peace and joy. The home is above all a place to be. It gives both the core members and the assistants a sense of belonging. This is especially important for the former, most of whom have suffered greatly from the lack of any experience of belonging somewhere and to someone. For many of them it is their first experience of having a home that they can call their own, and where they do not have to measure up to brighter brothers and sisters, or to more conforming residents in some institution. This is seen in the importance they give to inviting guests – from one of the other homes or from elsewhere – to come to their home for dinner. The newly arrived assistants quickly realize that it is they who must accommodate themselves to the men and women with disabilities in the homes. It is very much their home, and the assistants have to learn to adapt to the lifestyle that the core members choose to create there.

Because they find in the homes a security and freedom to be themselves, the core members often manifest a joy that springs from their simplicity and purity of heart. The privileged moment for expressing this joy is at the meal, the one time of the day when all are together. So the "liturgy" of the meal is very important. The singing of grace before and a thanksgiving afterward help to convey something of the sacredness of this moment of encounter. The meals are seldom rushed, and sometimes the evening meal will be prolonged in a kind of spontaneous celebration as people, caught up in the joy of being together, begin singing and rejoicing in one form or another. One evening, for example, when I was at Valinos for supper, we got going with all the instruments we could find in the house – tambourines, triangles, bells, and finally with knives and forks tapping on plates, glasses, and serving dishes – until everyone at the table was making their contribution to the "music." Also, every birthday and feast day is an occasion to celebrate and for everyone in the home to say to the person whose feast it is how much he or she is loved and appreciated, thus deepening their sense of belonging and others' appreciation of them.

Such moments are opportunities for individuals to perform, to experience the joy of making others happy. In the home of l'Arche, Trosly, on almost every one of these occasions, Raphaël would be invited to play or sing. He usually began by protesting vigorously, looking at his watch and insisting that it was terribly late and that he had more important things to do elsewhere. His watch, of course, would almost certainly not have the correct time if it was running at all, but this made no difference since Raphaël had no idea how to tell time. His watch served an important function that had nothing to do with knowing the time. In any case, sooner or later Raphaël would leave the dining room grumpily pointing to his watch. A few minutes later he would come back in, wearing a big smile and carrying a large plastic shopping bag. He would begin digging into the bag and pulling out various kinds of flutes and horns, finally handing his music score to his neighbor to hold for him. If it was a woman, as it usually was, he would give her a gentle hug or at least a loving pat on the top of the head. Raphaël had all the gestures of a temperamental virtuoso, so much so that any guests witnessing this scene for the first time might well expect that they were about to be treated to an exquisite auditory experience. They might, however, become a bit suspicious if they took a good look at the music score and knew enough French to realize that it was simply a handbill that had recently been left at the door to announce the bargain rates being offered at the general store. There would be much chattering and laughing in the dining room; Raphaël, standing poised with his favorite instrument, a strange-looking green-and-white plastic flute, would wait impatiently for total silence and attention. He might only at this moment have realized that he had been holding his instrument upside down or backwards, and the necessary adjustment would be made without the slightest sign of embarrassment. Then, with an air of gravity and intense concentration, he would begin to play. The sounds that issued forth are indescribable, a weird, shrieking music that reduced everyone to tears of laughter. As often as I heard Raphaël play this instrument, my response was always one of delightful surprise. Throughout the performance he maintained his serious composure, with only the glint in his eyes indicating how much he was enjoying it all.

What is most impressive on these occasions is the way Raphaël, George, Jacques, and the others are called forth by the community to give of themselves and their particular talent. George's repertoire consists of only one song, and yet everyone in his home is eager to have him sing on these occasions and earnestly coaxes him to do so. He is a heavy, brooding person who does not always respond positively to this coaxing. When he does condescend to perform, no one is bored by hearing the same old song. There is great delight in seeing George come out of himself in this way with the evident satisfaction he takes in being able to be the center of attention for a few minutes. Pierrot, on the other hand, hardly has to be coaxed to sing. He will, almost invariably, have memorized a new song for every feast day or birthday that comes along. In a way, what takes place during these celebrations is what the community is trying to realize in its whole way of life: to call forth the best in each individual and help them to discover and realize more fully their own potential.

This works in two ways. The group, by its attitude of respect and assurance, gives individuals the needed confidence to express themselves; the individuals, by giving whatever they are capable of, supply encouragement to the rest of the group. When Yves, with his harelip that makes his speech practically impossible to decipher, has the courage to get up and sing for us, it challenges all of us to "let our light shine before others," however tentative that light may be.

Two particular aspects of these celebrations in the homes are worth underlining: the way they can go on even in spite of the fact that many who are involved might be suffering considerably, and the way they flow so easily into prayer. A typical example that highlights both these aspects was one evening at the home of l'Arche, when several of the women from Valinos were invited for supper and an evening get-together.

After supper we gathered in the living room, some 30 of us crowded together on the floor around a few lighted candles. Pierrot, our music expert, had prepared the program, but while he was out of the room rounding up the last of the crowd, the singing began without him, though Pierrot soon took things in hand. One of the first things on the program was a game presented by Christian. Christian, who is usually fairly heavy and serious, manifested another side of his character as he playfully demonstrated the game: a lit cigarette dangling by a thread from the front of the brim of a straw hat. The trick is to get the cigarette into the mouth (preferably not the lit end) without using the hands, but merely by tilting the head or blowing on the cigarette. First Pierrot tried it, and to the delight of everyone was completely defeated by the dangling cigarette. Albert next tried and managed it with no difficulty. Then Dédé gave it a try, which brought the evening almost to a standstill. Dédé takes such games with deadly seriousness, and once he gets started on something it is not easy to get him off it. He went on and on, and we all got more and more restless until someone got up the courage to gently take the hat from him and pass it to the next participant. Those who know Dédé well breathed a sigh of relief to see that he took this defeat rather easily. He proved this later on in the evening when he condescended to sing a solo – a rare and wonderful event, because he sings in a voice that is barely audible but hauntingly moving.

Everyone seemed to especially enjoy seeing Jean Vanier and myself try the hat game, judging from all the laughter and applause.

So the evening continued with group songs, solos, guitar music, and much laughter. Several of the women, who were quite sullen and obviously in a state of anguish during the meal, seemed to relax and join in the fun, with the exception of Laura, who had been raving or laughing hysterically since the beginning of the evening. She gave such competition to Marie's beautiful solo that the latter with her gentle voice was finally reduced to silence. But Jean Vanier turned the moment into a joke by calling for a round of applause, first for Marie and then for Laura. Everyone laughed, including the two women. Jean has developed to a fine art the use of humor to defuse explosive situations. As the evening wore on, the atmosphere became more peaceful and the songs more religious. The turning point was the singing of Psalm 150, "Bless the Lord, All You Works of the Lord," with people spontaneously offering different verses: "All the girls of Valinos, bless the Lord," "Burning candles, bless the Lord," "Jean Vanier, bless the Lord," and so forth. It continued on joyfully until everyone in the room had been named, as well as all the different homes of Trosly and centers of l'Arche elsewhere in the world.

All through the evening Gilles had been courageously fighting a state of depression. Finally, he got weakly to his feet, took a step to cross the room toward the door, and vomited up his supper, partly on the floor and partly on Bruce's back. One of the assistants was immediately at Gilles's side to help him out of the room. Bruce slipped out to change his shirt, and two others began to clean up the floor, while everyone else remained calmly in their places going on with the singing with hardly a hesitation, all with a naturalness of people accustomed to such things.

At the singing of "Les Mains Ouvertes Devant Toi, Seigneur," everyone held out their hands in a sign of offering. (On a similar occasion in another home, it had been Ange who requested that they sing this song. Ange has a history of incredible suffering. When he was young, his hands and face were severely burned. Those who were supposed to be looking after him gave no attention to his burns, and his fingers were finally all lost. So Ange had nothing but his gnarled stubs to hold out as he sang, "My hands are open before you, Lord, to offer you the world," yet an inner radiance transformed his badly scarred face into something angelic.) Finally, a profound stillness pervaded the room. After a long moment of silence, Jean Vanier began to pray aloud, thanking Jesus for this evening and commending to his loving care so many lonely people in the world who do not experience this kind of joy and friendship. A couple of other people added their prayers; another long, prayerful silence followed, and all joined hands to sing the Our Father. Everyone shared a few joyful moments of leave-taking and saying good night, hugging and shaking hands.

Sometimes these gatherings in the homes would have a specifically religious orientation. Once a month there was a "spiritual weekend," at which time Père Thomas used to give a conference and one of the homes prepared an evening get-together. These weekends could coincide with important liturgical feasts, but in any case often included a "vigil" (a prayerful get-together) on the eve of the more important feasts.

On the eve of the departure of a group going on pilgrimage to La Salette, a vigil was held at La Source. This home, being the former village hotel, has a large living room, easily accommodating the 60 to 70 people who came for this particular evening.

We were all spread in a large circle, two or three rows deep, to leave the center of the room clear. After an opening song, the scene of the apparition at La Salette of the Blessed Virgin to the two children, Maximin and Mélanie, was acted out. These evenings often feature such a presentation, carried out with a certain seriousness but including some humor as well, intentional or otherwise. When Maximin and Mélanie came into the room driving their cows before them there was so much laughter that we could hardly hear Hubert, who was narrating the scene. The "cows" were half a dozen men on all fours, with blankets or sacks thrown over them to make them look a little bit like cows, or at least a little less like men on all fours. When Maximin and Mélanie fell asleep, the cows wandered off. Five of the six managed to find the kitchen door and to disappear from the scene, but the sixth cow had his blanket too far over his eyes to see where he was going. After wandering around the room for a minute or so, with everyone happily trying to point him in the right direction, this cow, in exasperation, stood up on his hind legs and slunk off to the kitchen – looking very much like a young man named Stephen. This all but stopped the show. Maximin and Mélanie awoke and began looking for their cows, when suddenly at the kitchen door there was the apparition! The Blessed Virgin stood there in her blue cloak bearing the gentle features of Daniel. A few giggles escaped, but there was something convincing in the very gentleness and shyness of Daniel. All he could do was whisper his one line, after being prompted from behind the kitchen door: "Do not be afraid, come here close to me." Perhaps Daniel's unique gift was to be so gentle and retiring as not to frighten even the most timid person. The scene ended with everyone singing the hymn to the Virgin of La Salette.

Then one of the assistants led a discussion on the question posed by the Blessed Virgin: "My children, do you say your prayers?" This discussion was an impressively honest search to discover the place of prayer in our daily lives. Another song, and then a time of prayer centered around the theme of fear and confidence ("Do not be afraid, come here close to me") was led by myself. The evening ended with a quiet hymn and a long moment of rich silence.

An extraordinary naturalness is found in this kind of prayerful encounter in the homes, where good humor and laughter readily find their place, and also in the way other festive gatherings almost always terminate in a prayerful spirit. This result seems to be a sign of the deep faith life in the community, which in turn seems to spring from the simplicity of heart that characterizes so many of its members. For most of the people at the heart of l'Arche, God and Jesus are deeply felt and unquestionable realities in their lives. They will talk easily about these matters at table, in the workshops, or during leisure moments. Even those, almost especially those, who have no habit of religious worship are eager to speak about these subjects, not by way of questioning their existence but rather to understand what this existence implies for their own lives.

It is at least partly because of this kind of faith that suffering – one's own and that of others – can be openly acknowledged and shared.

Of course, the very density of the suffering that is there makes it difficult not to acknowledge at least some of it, and the intensity of the interpersonal relations makes it difficult not to share in one another's suffering. Out of this acknowledgment and sharing of suffering comes a sense of communion that is supportive and liberating. Together we can look at our suffering for what it is, accept it, even laugh about it. This kind of communion has a peculiar depth and honesty, because suffering tends to touch us at the deepest level of our being, and contains a kind of unavoidable and undeniable veracity.

Such a communion is then a real communion of persons, and this person-to-person encounter is a joyful experience. It is joyful in the profoundest sense of that term, the kind of joyfulness that can co-exist with great suffering. This joyfulness permeates the life at l'Arche, occasionally bursting forth in spontaneous celebration as well as being nurtured and encouraged by organized celebrations. Such celebration does not need the catalysts of alcohol, drugs, or sexual indulgence, all of which tend to impede, not enhance, personal communion. Rather, it is the simple expression of the joy of personal communion, a communion that calls individuals out of themselves, liberating them from the isolation of self-pity and from the fear of death that is implicit in all suffering. At least momentarily one is liberated from suffering and self-centeredness in being caught up in something that springs from these but goes beyond them. However fleeting this experience might be, it conveys at least in some vague and preconceptual way the possibility of a final and total liberation in a communion that is without limit. So this kind of celebration points toward and calls for a ritual expression that makes explicit all that is implied here, a communion that is an experience of liberation and hope and a promise of fulfillment in an eternal celebration. There exists, then, an intimate connection between the kinds of celebration that take place in the homes and the liturgical life that goes on in the chapel, central to which is the celebration of the Eucharist.

Worship, as we saw earlier, is a focal point in the community's life. Individuals are brought to and are united at the Eucharist, in and through a common awareness of their poverty and suffering. Yet the Eucharist is above all a celebration. The important religious feasts are usually anticipated, prepared for, and celebrated with due solemnity. Well, "solemnity" is perhaps not the ideal word to describe what transpires at these services, either on feast days or on a daily basis. No matter what preparations may be made in advance, a kind of spontaneity and surprise element are always introduced by the most innocent members of the congregation, turning every Eucharist into a kind of "happening." But for all this, it is still a very prayerful event.

The spirit of acceptance that is such a vital part of l'Arche's lifestyle is evident here in the community chapel. Singing is part of almost every Eucharist, because singing seems to be the unique way of praying for some of the core members, and there are a few who simply must sing in order to express their uncontainable joy at certain moments of the service. However, no one feels obliged to sing. There are always enough enthusiasts to carry the singing, so those who prefer to participate more silently are perfectly free to do so. Besides, there are usually a few people at the Eucharist who are simply physically incapable of speaking, let alone singing, while there are sometimes others too burdened for the moment to be able to utter a sound. But these people find a real welcome and support here close to the altar, with friends who understand and accept their silence and, at times, their tears. As a student who spent the summer there observed:

> One of the things I really liked at l'Arche was that I could be with the other people and not be forced to sing and dance and clap my hands and so forth....You felt the community around you whether you were singing with them, praying out loud with them or not – the fact is you were all in the chapel praying, and there is a real community sense in that....The thing is that there, well, the difference from where I am now is that they didn't question – if you didn't sing, fine. It didn't make anybody uncomfortable. But it does here. So that's one of the things I found good there: you are just who you are. They have a simple way of accepting people just as they are.

In many ways the form of worship at Trosly is traditional and ordinary. Père Thomas himself had a great love for tradition and keenly desired to be faithful to the dictates of the hierarchy and liturgical commission. Also, he read assiduously the public addresses and other pronouncements of the pope, which he often quoted in his homilies and conferences.

It is here especially that an important aspect of the community's ecclesial dimension can be seen. The relationship to the hierarchy is juridical only in the sense that it has a priest chaplain. Père Thomas was very much a part of the life and spirit of the community, and was known, loved, and respected by all. He in turn had a great respect and fidelity to the local bishop and to the pope. Many in the community, partly due to Père Thomas's example but for other reasons as well, also have a personal love for the bishop and the pope. The bishop comes to Trosly at least once or twice a year to say Mass and share in some sort of party afterward, and every year or two comes to confer the sacrament of confirmation on several members of the community. For many at l'Arche, and especially the core members, he is not just *the* bishop but *our* bishop. This same kind of personal reference is also experienced toward the pope. L'Arche has made several pilgrimages to Rome. On the first, in 1965, the pilgrims had a private audience with the pope. A photograph of this event could be seen on the wall of a living room, dining room, or bedroom in almost every one of the homes at Trosly. For years afterward, many would recall this event with enthusiasm, and the words that the pope addressed to them were often quoted with feeling: "You, too, are called to be saints." On the second pilgrimage to Rome, four years later, they did not meet the pope privately but with some 10,000 other pilgrims from the four corners of the world. This was, nonetheless, a very personal encounter with their pope, who addressed to them personally several words of encouragement, who warmly embraced Jean Vanier, and who, in leaving the basilica, came expressly and only to their section and shook as many hands as he could reach. Among other things, he said to them,

We rejoice to see such a work being realized at l'Arche, under the direction of Mr. Jean Vanier. We congratulate all those who are working together there with dedication, in a spirit that is perfectly familial.... We would like to have a personal contact with each one of you. May you at least have, in the midst of this great Catholic family, a chosen place....

This trip included driving through the breathtaking Swiss Alps, seeing the marvels of Rome, outings to the beach and other festivities; yet afterward most of the men and women claimed that the highlight of the trip was seeing the pope. (This has taken us a little off the point, but it seems fitting in speaking about the life of worship to say a word about the community's relationship to the hierarchy, since this relationship is primarily experienced and expressed in and through the Eucharist.)

Indeed, there is something traditional and almost common-place about the community worship at Trosly. It is a daily, routine event like the evening meal that it normally precedes. But like the evening meal, it is a celebration open to the spontaneous expression of a whole gamut of human experiences. Even if the Sunday and feast-day services are prepared for with some special care, here too there is a spontaneous and unreflective participation. No one asks themselves or others, during or afterward, if this is or was a good liturgy. Having a "good liturgy" is not really the issue. All that really matters is to be together to worship God.

What follows is the description of one of those worship services that is as typical as such an event can be. André bursts into the chapel by the back door and, like a wild horse, dashes across to the sacristy on the other side. He tears open the sacristy door and disappears inside, slamming the door behind him. All the while he has been mumbling frantically that he must see Père Thomas. None of the dozen or more people in the back pews who must certainly have been disturbed, not to mention trampled upon, seem at all surprised at this passage of a tornado on two legs. Nor can anyone slow up André in time to point out to him that Père Thomas is right there at the altar, since the service has already begun. So a minute later the sacristy door opens gently and a subdued André reappears with a puzzled look on his long, gaunt face. Seeing that the service is already in progress, he continues standing there scratching his head for a moment, and then plunges back into the sacristy. A few minutes later he reappears with an alb draped over his large, gangling frame.

The term "alb," which is from the Latin word for white, is something of a misnomer for this vestment that André is wearing to assist in the services. Its whiteness has been irretrievably lost to the forces of dirt and disorder that prevail in the chaotic little sacristy, and tend to spill out into the chapel itself. With a couple of great strides André is at the front of the chapel. At the age of 20 he is only slowly bringing his long, awkward body under some control. He plops himself down on the stool beside me, where I am sitting next to the altar listening to Père Thomas. I, too, am in priestly vestments, since I am concelebrating with him. André gives me a warm smile as he extends his hand in greeting. As we shake hands, he says to me in simple sincerity, "I'm so happy that you're here." His presence to me is a Real Presence, one that makes me suddenly much more aware of why we are all here in the chapel.

André now begins taking inventory of the congregation, which numbers about 40. He nods and smiles at anyone whose eye he happens to catch. Having completed this task he turns back to me and, noticing my bowed head and drooping shoulders, he gently clasps my arm and asks, "How's it going? Tired?" When I nod in affirmation, his eyes fill with compassion and he gives me a soothing pat on the head. For all his brusqueness and lack of self-control, he has an extraordinary sensitivity to others.

Now the door next to the altar opens and Pierrot comes in for the third time since the beginning of the service. He stands there hesitatingly, wondering where to sit, until his friend Michel waves to him from the other side of the chapel. So he starts across the chapel by the narrow space between the altar and the front pew. He does his best to be unobtrusive, but trips over the feet of several people and jostles the wooden altar behind which Père Thomas is standing. The latter goes on preaching without the slightest sign of any disturbance. Pierrot gives me a huge smile as he goes by. As he passes Josiane, who runs the home where he lives, he leans down and plants a kiss on the top of her head, his face radiating love and joy. Then he squeezes in beside Michel, and the two of them exchange several words before giving their attention to Père Thomas. Soon they are following him with rapt attention.

Sitting toward the middle of the chapel is a young woman from Valinos whom I baptized a few weeks earlier. She catches my eye and begins communicating to me with silently moving lips and gestures, telling me that she is in a state of anguish, that she intends to or has again cut herself on the wrists, and that she does not intend to receive Holy Communion today. From beside me, André blows her a kiss and then indicates that she should keep still.

During the prayers of the faithful, a number of people speak up, asking prayers for deceased relatives, for friends who have left l'Arche, for flood victims in Egypt, for Asha Niketan and the people of India, and so forth. When Jean-Claude prays that Gilbert, who coordinates the house in which Jean-Claude lives, be made more kindly, everyone smiles broadly, especially Gilbert himself. Patrick D. lifts his angelic face from the comic book he has been thumbing all through the Mass, raises his long, bony arm to get Père Thomas's attention, and says abruptly, "For my parents." A gentle smile crosses his face, but it is soon lost from sight as he returns his attention to the comic book.

The singing might not be perfect, but it does testify to a lively conviction. Several of the men close to the altar are tone deaf. Their loud, raspy voices give me courage to lend my own poor voice to the singing, but also make it a challenge to remain anywhere close to the correct note and key.

At the moment in the service when we are invited to show one another that we are at peace together, the chapel comes alive in an extraordinary way. Some people shake hands not just with their immediate neighbor, but with everyone they can reach in all directions. A few even leave their places to go and greet someone for whom at the moment they may have some special feeling. Even those few people who, until this time, seemed to have been totally lost in prayer now come alive with a radiant smile for those close to them. André, after receiving the sign of peace from me at the altar, works his way to the back corner of the chapel, shaking hands with many on each side of the narrow aisle, until he reaches his dearest friend, one of the assistants, a fragile woman who has been in tears throughout the service. He reaches down to where she is kneeling on the stone floor, takes her hand and gently kisses it; then, patting her on the head, he offers a few words of comfort before awkwardly barging back toward the front of the chapel.

At communion time almost everyone files by the altar to receive the Bread of Life. Some join in the singing, while others seem absorbed in prayer. Gerard gives great attention to the music book he is holding upside-down and sings with unintelligible sounds. He gives Père Thomas and me a big smile, then adopts an attitude of profound respect as he receives communion. They file by, one by one, and the chapel is illuminated by the joyful tone of the singing and the peace that can be seen in many of their faces.

After communion comes a moment of profound stillness. Then Père Thomas says the closing prayer and gives the blessing, and priests and servers head for the sacristy as the final hymn is sung with great enthusiasm. The sacristy is a scene of confusion as several little children, as well as a few of the men and women with disabilities and assistants, come crowding in while the priests and servers are still trying to remove their liturgical vestments. They come to see – or to make an appointment to see – the chaplain, or to ask for a little statue or holy card or rosary, or simply to greet us with a friendly handshake, as Benoit never fails to do after every service.

The village square outside the chapel suddenly takes on an air of festivity. People greet one another as though they had not met for ages, or say goodbye as though they were separating for months and not just until the next day. The women from Valinos climb into cars to drive the two miles back to their village. The fellows and assistants from Pierrefond, three miles away, shouting and singing, climb into "Gougousse," the double-decker English bus that still bears the names of the London streets it used to travel before being whisked away to France and finally donated to l'Arche. Gougousse lumbers off like a giant red elephant with its happy occupants waving out the windows and singing a rousing chorus of "Allé-allé-alléluia." With the departure of Gougousse, the square takes on its usual evening serenity, and the remaining people, mostly in groups of twos and threes, head toward their homes in the village to have their dinner. Variations on this scene are repeated every day after the service, only with a noticeable increase in the numbers and intensity on feast days and Sundays.

When two or more priests happen to be at l'Arche, another Eucharist may be held, often in the late evening, for the benefit of a few who cannot get to the community service or who may at times prefer a quieter liturgy. These services are held in the little chapel of La Ferme, a center for prayer and reflection, and are usually carried on in a spirit of intense prayerfulness, with extended periods of silent or shared prayer. Yet here, too, is found a sense of celebration that springs from a deeply felt awareness of a communion in a common enterprise and a common faith vision, as well as in a mutual sharing of one another's sufferings and joys.

This experience of communion at community worship is grounded in hope and is a source of hope. The awareness of one's own pain or loneliness or limitations is systematically avoided if there is no hope of transcending them in some way, or else this awareness leads toward despair. Only with some hope of transcendence can such limitations in oneself or in others be simply faced and accepted. For this reason, at least in part, the Eucharist, the celebration of the passage through death to life, is the pre-eminent milieu where the people of l'Arche are brought together in the deepest kind of acceptance of their suffering and limitations, and hence the profoundest kind of awareness of one another. It is precisely in worship that the distinction between the people with disabilities and the assistants vanishes. Here, each person appears in all his or her uniqueness as a child of God, redeemed by the death and resurrection of Jesus, and is called into a personal relationship with God in and through Jesus. The communion that is experienced is a communion between persons on a level of equality. The ritual here is not, as it sometimes can be, a way of protecting the minister and congregation from any truly human encounter. A real encounter of people makes communion more than just a liturgical expression. Here André can both greet and console the minister, and Jane can express her state of anguish without concern for what others may think; an assistant can let her tears flow and be comforted by one of the men, Pierrot can express his love for Josiane, and Jean-Claude can express his disappointment with Gilbert.

Such an experience of communion is in itself an experience of transcending one's own suffering and limitations. It is an affirmation of a present reality that brings together the personal and collective history of all and relates it to the personal action of God in history, the incarnation of God in Jesus and his suffering, death, and resurrection. As St. Paul says, "As often as you eat this bread and drink this cup, you proclaim the death of the Lord until he comes" (1 Corinthians 11:23). It is a "doing" and a "proclaiming," a being in the present with the awareness of death, the death of Jesus and one's own death as it is intimated in one's own suffering and the suffering of others. It is also a pointing to the future, to the coming of the Lord. But this coming of the Lord is not purely future, not purely eschatological. The very experience of communion with others in hope is an experience of transcendent love breaking through the barriers of one's own limitations and the barriers that separate people from one another. This is implicitly an experience of the God of Love coming into our world. It was at the Eucharist that Robert broke through the barrier of fear that had kept him unable to speak for two weeks after his arrival at La Merci. His first words were "I love Jesus."

One final aspect of the life of celebration at l'Arche needs to be considered: the pilgrimage. Each year since the beginning of l'Arche has included a community pilgrimage. Besides making trips to Rome, in other years three separate groups have traveled to

Lourdes, Fatima, or La Salette, and more recently to England and Poland. The pilgrimage is not just a religious experience, a going together as a community to a place of prayer and worship to pray and worship together; it is also very much a vacation trip. This is especially important for many of the people, for whom the holiday month of August spent with relatives is anything but a vacation. So each one in the community is free to choose to make one of these trips in the spring of the year.

Perhaps one of the important aspects of the yearly pilgrimage is the experience of freedom and liberation that is expressed by this kind of adventure. For one thing, the considerable risk involved inspires an honest dependence on providence. To take a risk is somehow to be liberated and to experience a new sense of freedom. The trip to Rome, for example, entailed all kinds of minor but real risks. It meant uprooting almost the entire community, close to 200 people, including those from La Merci, Ambleteuse, and Valinos. It meant putting more than 20 vehicles on the road for the three-day trip across France and part of Switzerland and Italy, driving around for a week in the frightfully chaotic traffic of Rome, and then spending three days driving home. With the exception of one rented bus, the only vehicles were those available in the communities, including a couple of fifteen-seat mini-buses that were living out their last days and two or three Deux Chevaux (a two-cylinder 30-horsepower car) that are great on downhill stretches but can be reduced almost to walking speed by a steep incline or even a strong headwind. They formed a motley caravan, spaced along the highways in groups of twos and threes, moving across the Alps towards Rome with all the daring and determination of Hannibal and his forces – but with greater success in conquering Rome with their love and laughter than he with his pride and power. Much would have been simplified could they have afforded to travel by train, plane, or chartered buses, yet much would have been lost with regard to the whole spirit of the trip. The departure ceremony began with an act of community worship, an early-morning Eucharist. Then Père Thomas, from the steps of the chapel, said a prayer and blessed the vehicles and their occupants – a blessing for which the need was felt intensely, especially by those in the mini-buses and Deux Chevaux.

Limited finances also imposed the necessity of finding cheap accommodations. Up until the last week before setting out, we were still praying and searching for 30 more beds for the week in Rome, and 80 beds for the one-night stopover in Geneva. Finally, a convent was procured by friends in Rome, and a friend in Geneva acquired the use of an army barracks, so we all breathed a sigh of relief and a prayer of thanksgiving. A certain kind of freedom comes when we travel with enough money to be able to afford whatever hotel space may be available, but anyone who has traveled with little more than a sleeping bag on their back and a smile on their face, as is the case with a vast number of today's youth, has probably discovered a deeper kind of freedom in this simplicity and dependence on providence. Also, we had to bring along enough provisions for a picnic lunch each day of the two-week journey, with the exception of bread and fruit, which were purchased fresh each day. So we were free to pull off the road by a mountain stream or in a wooded grove or on one of the seven hills of Rome with the city spread out beneath us, and share our sandwiches of canned meat and cheese, our canned vegetables and fresh fruit in a spirit of joyful simplicity.

This pilgrimage to Rome, like all the pilgrimages, was thoroughly prepared for by everyone. All those making the trip were divided into groups of 25 or 30. These groups met once a week for about six weeks prior to departure. They met to consider the practical aspects of the trip, but especially to better understand the cultural and spiritual significance of this journey. Together we studied the maps of France, Switzerland, Italy, and Rome. We studied the Rome of the Caesars, the Rome of the martyrs, and the Rome of the successors of St. Peter. We learned a few Italian words and expressions, saw slides of the monuments, sang and prayed, all in an exuberant spirit of expectation.

The trips to Lourdes, Fatima, and La Salette are prepared for in a similar way. The reason these three shrines have a special attraction for l'Arche is not difficult to discern. Each owes its origin to an apparition of the Virgin Mary to poor and innocent children. As a result of these apparitions, thousands of people go there yearly; among them are many who are sick and needy. Christians with an innocent faith, like so many at l'Arche, have a particular devotion to Jesus of Nazareth, especially to his infancy, childhood, and death on the cross. His life of preaching, his words and ideas, his risen life as Lord of history would have greater appeal to the more educated and the more sophisticated. Consequently, the people of l'Arche have a special devotion to the Mother of Jesus, who gave birth to him and nourished him in Bethlehem, who raised him in Nazareth, and who stood by him on Calvary. While the overly sophisticated may be scandalized at the thought of a devotion to Mary, the innocent find in her an all-important channel for coming into contact with the person of her Son. The people of l'Arche find it meaningful and helpful to place themselves and their communities under the protection of Jesus's mother. For a believer to be able to relate in some way to this innocent Jewish girl in whom the Word became flesh is a kind of touchstone of his or her simplicity. That the Virgin should appear to poor and innocent children has a great appeal to many at l'Arche.

In one of the group meetings in preparation for a trip to Lourdes, Dédé was spellbound by the realization that Mary had appeared to an ordinary person like himself. In fact, he simply could not see why he himself should not be similarly favored. He kept whispering over and over again, "The Blessed Virgin appeared to Bernadette, but she hasn't appeared to me!" I could not help feeling that it was just a question of time before she did, since Dédé, in spite of, or perhaps because of, what psychiatry calls a profound autism, seems to be something of a mystic. He would stand gazing at the stars all night long if someone did not insist that he go to bed. On this trip to Lourdes, when they stopped to visit some friends in a cloistered Carmelite convent, seeing the iron grill that separated them from the sisters whose faces were radiant with an inner peace and joy, Dédé exclaimed, "*C'est le prison de l'esperance!*" [It is the prison of hope!]

Finally, at these shrines one encounters numerous sick people, many of whom are on stretchers or in wheelchairs. This encounter with suffering seems to touch something deep within the l'Arche members, calling from them an extraordinary capacity for compassion. While there, they do all they can to be of service to the sick, and long after these trips they continue to remember and pray for the many unfortunate people they have met. Here is what some of them had to say several weeks after their trip to Lourdes. "I need to pray very much for the sick. We must not forget them." "The sick are the ones who bring much comfort to us, the healthy. They revive us." "The sick people we saw there somehow made me feel sad. It bothers me to see them that way.... I was struck by the kindness and gentleness of the sick." Faced with those less fortunate than themselves, they quickly forget themselves and their own difficulties.

Many good things come out of making a pilgrimage together as a community, including the communal experience of a dependence on providence; the coming together in groupings different than those that occur in the daily routine of life, and living in the even closer intimacy that such a trip necessitates; the broadening of vision that comes with seeing other parts of the country and the continent and meeting other peoples; the deeper realization of their own unique esprit de corps, especially through the experience of bringing comfort, joy, and hope to many whom they meet. Finally, the pilgrimage is just an overall good and enriching experience that helps to open the person in the depths of his or her sensibilities. This, in itself, is a liberating experience that, in some deep-seated and implicit way, calls forth a greater sense of one's own potentiality for life, a greater hope. Furthermore, since the whole or a large part of the community shares this enriching experience, it gives to the whole community a greater sense of its potentiality to live a fuller and richer life together, a greater hope in the community itself.

These yearly pilgrimages are a kind of ritual expression or celebration of the whole life and spirit of l'Arche, which help to bring to the participants' own awareness just what this spirit is. They are a fragile little flock of people on the move together. Living in the kind of risk that such a fragility implies, they are forced to radically depend on one another and on the Lord of Life. This they do with an innocent faith that makes little or no distinction between the sacred and the secular: birthday parties slide into worship, worship services are festive parties, and the pilgrimage itself is both a religious event and a holiday with lots of fun. For, fundamentally, all life is sacred, a truth that becomes more evident as life is reduced to its simpler necessities, and especially as suffering and death are squarely faced and accepted. So life is celebrated at l'Arche in a spirit of abandonment that springs from an awareness of their poverty as individuals and as a community, and from an awareness of the sacred mystery of life itself.

The unique values of the l'Arche spirit are brought home to its members in a special way in making this kind of trip together. They discover that their style of life has meaning not only within the usual context of their little village but elsewhere as well – in traveling and in such different contexts as the remote mountains of La Salette and in great cities. Their way of living more fully in the present moment takes on a heightened significance when, for example, they are caught in an enormous traffic jam in the heart of Rome. Then their singing and joy become a celebration of their liberation from the external pressure of competitive, technological society, and a desire to bring some liberation to those around them who are likewise caught in the stagnant ocean of vehicles. "We are not going to get out of here for some time, so let us just enjoy being here." What other response could one expect from a group with its Dédés, who can be ecstatic over the beauty of a shattered windshield? And with its Moniques, who can accept the death of a beloved brother painfully but with an extraordinary peace and joy that spring from a certainty that he is now with the Lord? So the stay in Rome was an experience of the way their own lifestyle gave them a kind of freedom that many others did not seem to have. Their lack of money, for example, made it clear that the admission fee to visit the Coliseum simply could not apply to them. So they sang and chanted and regaled the attendants until the latter happily allowed them to enter free of charge. In visiting the ruins of the ancient Roman port of Ostia, here again the admittance fee was waived due to the group's insistence expressed in song and laughter. This was helped by some uniquely Italian diplomacy carried on by our friend Henry, who has mastered both the language and histrionics of that country. The beautiful amphitheater of Ostia, with its grassy floor stretched out beneath the deep-blue Italian sky, did not invite these pilgrims to study the architecture or take photos like typical tourists, but to break into a spontaneous folk dance. Jean Vanier himself became boyishly immersed in the fun, like someone who had not the slightest care in the world.

I do not wish to imply scorn for people who are immersed in a competitive, technological society; nor do I wish to imply that the people of l'Arche are totally liberated from such a society. But to celebrate life in the face of the burdens of existence is to experience at least the beginning of a true liberation, and to declare for oneself and for others a hope that is grounded in the preciousness of life and the undying worth of the human person. It is this kind of celebration that Henri Nouwen qualifies as being truly Christian:

> When we speak about celebration we tend rather easily to bring to mind happy, pleasant, gay festivities in which we can forget for a while the hardships of life and immerse ourselves in an atmosphere of music, dance, drinks, laughter, and a lot of cozy small-talk. But celebration in the Christian sense has very little to do with this. Celebration is only possible through the deep realization that life and death are never found completely separate. Celebration can only really come about where fear and love, joy and sorrow, tears and smiles can exist together. Celebration is the acceptance of life in a constantly increasing awareness of its preciousness. And life is precious not only because it can be seen, touched, and tasted, but also because it will be gone one day.[9]

8

How to Build Your Own Ark

Sometime after I had left Trosly to resume a different way of life in Canada, someone asked me if I missed l'Arche. My spontaneous answer surprised even me: "I'm still at l'Arche." This truth has grown on me. After experiencing this community, in one sense we always remain a part of it. L'Arche is not a place, but a way of life.

Although much has been said in these pages about this new type of community, it is really quite simple and ordinary. This very fact is what prevents those who have lived there from ever leaving it completely. In essence, l'Arche is a group of ordinary people living an intense life of personal relationships. Once people have entered into this way of life, they are held in it by bonds of friendship even though they may be separated by distance or activity. Furthermore, a life of deep personal relationships can be lived almost anywhere. There is no need to go to Trosly or any other of the l'Arche centers to find this. The fundamental meaning of l'Arche is that community is a gift offered to me where I am. It begins with the recognition of the uniqueness of myself and each of those around me and the commitment to overcome the barriers that separate us so that we can celebrate life together.

Ordinary it is, yet people leaving l'Arche invariably experience considerable difficulty resuming life in our society. This fact perhaps reveals more about our society than it does about l'Arche. One young woman who had lived there for almost a year says,

I think the biggest thing for me was that I found so many of what I feel are really true relationships, really deep relationships. It was something different for me. I had time to really think about life, what it was. I thought I knew all about it; well, I've been to university and I had all the answers. I found that until I changed somewhat I couldn't really communicate with those people. You have to throw off a lot of your former ideas. It was kind of funny – because you're busy working all the time and yet that's when I had time to think, when I was really busy. You're with these people all the time and you question it, you know – Why am I doing this? Why are they doing this? There must be a reason. Well, when I really started to think is when I realized I was so happy – and then you look at your surroundings and it's completely foreign to what most of us Canadians have, and you can't help but wonder – well, there must be something deeper here.

The transition is often spoken of in terms of having been more fully alive at l'Arche than one can easily be elsewhere. One man says, "When I got back to Canada many of the things we talked about and did were just not that important. [At l'Arche] I felt more involved with living." Another speaks in similar terms:

> I noticed a real change when I got back [to Canada]. Things seemed so artificial, almost. I felt like I was being kind of forced into a – a world of make-believe. Because at Trosly I found I could really just be myself, and be pretty relaxed. But back here you get all these outside pressures on you, and it just felt artificial.

The community of l'Arche has given people a greater fullness of life that sensitizes them to the aspects of our society that tend to diminish life, to dehumanize rather than humanize.

All of these people struggle to come to terms with this conflict. The tension is resolved for some by their sharing in other forms of community that continue to sustain them. Some have begun or joined l'Arche communities elsewhere, or have simply returned to Trosly. Others do manage to take up their former way of life, but usually there is a difference. For example, a lawyer and his family returned to their home and work after spending a year at Trosly but, as they told me, were much less concerned about success or failure and better able to live more simply. A few people, even several years later, are still unsettled and in search of a way of life that can satisfy them. What I have found especially remarkable in meeting so many of these people is that, no matter how difficult the transition might be for them, none conclude that they should not have gone to Trosly. Even people who found the life difficult and were unhappy there, after leaving l'Arche they look back on it as an enriching experience. As much as they may have felt out of place at l'Arche, they still have the problem of this transition back into "normal" society. So which of these ways of living is truly more normal?

The kind of tension that is experienced by men and women leaving l'Arche is by no means limited to them. The dehumanizing aspects of our society are being more acutely experienced by most people. They increasingly hunger for the joy that comes from the freedom of being more oneself, of being more fully alive. L'Arche is one indication that such joy can still be had. It is a message of hope proclaiming that there is an alternative to submitting to those aspects of our society that negate this joy by turning people in on themselves.

This, of course, is not to say that the contrast is black and white, with people finding great wholeness through l'Arche and little or no human fulfillment in our technological society; technology offers immense benefits for the whole of humankind. Certainly the l'Arche communities have no monopoly on joy and freedom, and most of them are well rooted in our technological society. The issue is more a question of the conditions that favor or militate against a greater fullness of human living, and the criteria by which these conditions can be recognized.

The conditions that favor a more human way of living are threatened in our society by the overpowering drive for a more comfortable way of living. Comfort, of course, is a good thing, but it can become a kind of ultimate value in a consumer society. And consume we must, at an ever-increasing rate. This is the very economic base on which technological society is presently constructed. The economy must continue to grow at a certain rate, so we must continue to increase production at a certain rate, and consequently must continue to increase consumption at that same rate. This rate of consumption is stimulated by a bombardment through the mass media, geared to convincing us of all the things we need and simply cannot live without. Products that were unheard of 20 years ago are things we supposedly cannot live without today. Furthermore, it is mathematically certain that with this economic base, the wealthy nations become ever more wealthy at the expense of the impoverished nations, which at best progress economically at a much slower rate. The whole system makes perfect sense in terms of the economic model on which it is based. However, looking at it from the viewpoint of human values and from a consideration of the entire human race, it is a kind of controlled insanity. It can only lead to human destruction and even the destruction of the planet.

In more lucid moments, most people sense the insanity of this way of life and the inevitable destruction to which it leads. But it is difficult to face this issue squarely when one is drowning in this world of consumption. Fearing the approach of death, we try to hide behind the walls of comforting goods that give us a sense that all is secure.

The security that comes from this world of comfort is really most tenuous, and actually leads to a worse death than the one that is being escaped. Human beings themselves are consumed in a world of consumer goods. Our lives are outside of ourselves in the wealth of goods that surround us. The call of mass-media advertising is a call away from the center of our being, pulling us out into all these false needs. We vacate our interior life and are left to wither and die.

Furthermore, we can easily become trapped in the ghetto of wealth and become terribly fearful of the poor who surround us. Then we cannot afford to hear the cry of the poor because responding would mean giving up the security of our wealth. Life speaks to life. Life calls forth life. If we can no longer hear the cries of the dying, this is regrettable – not because it is a failure of justice and love, but because it means we are dying. It means that there is no life in us to respond to the life that cries out for help. As a Jesuit priest working with the poor in the Philippines once said to me, "It's a life-death struggle everywhere, but death by consumerism is such a comfortable death."

Of course, much valid pleasure may be experienced in the world of consumer goods, but little deep joy. The pleasure is usually short-lived, and often gives way to the pain of boredom.

Being caught up in a world of false needs makes it more and more difficult to discover true and basic human needs. So the deeper meaning of human existence becomes ever more obscure.

The joy at l'Arche springs from two factors that oppose consumption and comfort: namely, simplicity and the acceptance of the reality of suffering. The simplicity of the people with developmental disabilities means that their lives are in fact reduced to the basics: the need for acceptance and love, the need to create, the need to find meaning for one's life. These needs are not lost in a cloud of lesser needs. Out of the search to fulfill these basic human needs is revealed most clearly what it means to be human. Interactions between people are not merely the exchange of goods and services, nor just a seeking of whatever pleasure might be in it for me. Interactions with people living on this level of simplicity necessarily become interpersonal, a giving and receiving of love and affection, and affirming and being affirmed as a person. Such relationships are never sterile but always productive of life. Work is not just a means of acquiring more comfort-goods. It has human fulfillment as its very purpose. It is a way of expressing the fundamental need to achieve and create, and provides a means by which people enter more deeply into interpersonal relationships. Finally, the life of worship responds to the need for meaning by allowing people to enter into a deeper relationship with other worshipers, with the whole cosmos, and with the Source and End of all creation.

In opposition to the emptying effect that comes from being drawn into a world of things exists the call from within – a call to stillness where we can come together at the center of our being to be nourished by the inner Source of existence. This call can perhaps be more easily heard in an atmosphere such as l'Arche, but it is even more needed in the turmoil of our consumer society. One man experienced this acutely:

> My big experience when I got back from l'Arche was a fantastic hunger – I mean it was physical – I ached inside. The only way I could get any relief was in prayer – only by going to the Eucharist or just going to the chapel and praying did I get relief from this tremendous hunger I felt inside me.

What all this tells us is that the conditions that favor a more fully human existence are those that allow us to live at the level of our most basic needs, and keep us from getting caught in a network of false needs that disperse and distract from the core of existence. We cannot avoid being a part of this consumer society, which contains much that is of value. But we can be sensitive to the criteria that lead us to a greater or lesser degree of freedom. Being more and more anxious for comfort is a sign that we are moving toward enslavement in the world of things. A bigger car, a bigger house, and more expensive tastes in clothing, food, and drink may all be fine, but they will not necessarily render us more fully alive. On the contrary, they may tend to distract us from the deeper meaning of our lives. They may also separate us more from our hungry brothers and sisters and so, finally, from what is most truly human within ourselves. To reject another is always a rejection of a part of oneself. Whatever moves us toward greater simplicity, on the other hand, will be indicative of a move toward greater wholeness. When we draw closer to identifying with the poorest of our society and of the world, we become ever more free from the fear that imprisons many in their riches. Meeting with the people at l'Arche has been for many not just the acceptance of the poverty of the other, but also the acceptance of their own poverty and so the freedom to be more themselves.

If comfort becomes an absolute, then suffering is the greatest evil and must be avoided at all costs. We thus flee suffering and death, but this flight is also a flight from reality, since suffering and death are an integral part of the reality of human existence. Suffering is, of course, an evil to be avoided, but not at all costs. It is an inevitable part of human existence, and so must at least be accepted when it cannot be eliminated. The more a society is based on comfort and pleasure, the more it must hide away its sick and aged and dying. The more a society loses touch with the reality of suffering and death, the more unreal and inhuman it becomes. Rarely now do people die in their homes surrounded by relatives. Death takes place in the isolation of a hospital, under so much sedation that it is even concealed from the person who is approaching it. Corpses are made to look like they are still alive. The very word "death" is replaced by euphemisms.

The inability to face suffering causes great barriers between individuals. If the man next to me is suffering and I am unable to accept suffering, then I can meet him only at the most superficial level, one that ignores a deep dimension of his existence. A profound bond of unity is created when two people can look at one another, see the suffering that is there and not turn away from it. The person who is suffering and dying is terribly alone and isolated. He or she can be comforted only by those who have come to terms with the reality of their own death and so are free to enter into this person's suffering and death. Others can only talk of banalities and try to cheer up the sick person, which will leave them feeling all the more alone and isolated. But there is a degree of suffering in everyone, so the "comfort society" tends to isolate us all. We have seen at l'Arche that there is a great deal of suffering. Jean Vanier often reminds us that l'Arche is founded on suffering. But this suffering is openly acknowledged and accepted, which leads to a deep communion between the people there, and to a real celebration of life and true joy. If comfort and pleasure are accepted as unique criteria of better living, they tend to lead away from what is more truly human. This can result in an escape into alcohol, drugs, sex, and violence if the pain of life becomes too threatening. On the other hand, what leads to a more honest acceptance of the reality of suffering and death will lead to a greater freedom to be oneself and to accept others. Trying to escape the reality of death results in a death of boredom and escapism. Accepting the reality of death leads to a more fully human existence, to true life, because it allows us to enter more deeply into the lives of others.

Underlying the fundamental attitude of life in a technological society is the drive for success. It gives rise to a competitive society in which one has no choice but to fight for a place in it. Even by the time a child has begun school, he or she has learned the need to succeed at all costs. Children are pushed to be the best in the classroom, on the playing field, and even in the area of socializing.

Out of this attitude of competition comes the fact that people are valued far more for what they can accomplish than for who they are. Doing is more important than being. This tends to cause a deep sense of alienation, because people are not valued for themselves but only for what they do. The drive to succeed can produce great things, but a sense of self-worth does not always come from it. Not only does this attitude alienate us within ourselves, it also tends to isolate us from others, because success usually comes at the expense of someone else's failure. Climbing the ladder of success means climbing over others who are less successful. The need for security forces people to play the game of competition, but real security is not to be had in success. People sense that just as success has been won at the expense of others, sooner or later they will be the victim of someone else more successful than they themselves. Where success is a kind of ultimate goal, even the most successful – in fact, *especially* the most successful – live in fear of falling from this lofty position.

A competitive society creates a kind of caste system. People are valued for what they do, so those who are more accomplished are more valued. Those who accomplish the least are the least respected. At the top of this caste system are the professional people, and at the bottom are such people as the elderly, alcoholics, people with disabilities, and so forth. The symbols of this caste system are a manner of dressing, a way of speaking, the places one frequents, and the like. How many of us respond with the same kind of openness to an elegantly dressed person stepping out of a chauffeured limousine, or to a man wearing a roman collar, or to a young person with long hair and jeans, or to someone who is dirty and shabbily dressed? Usually we react with fear to one type of person or another.

Related to this categorizing of people is the need to conform, the need to do what one in my position is expected to do. If I fail to conform, I will lose my position, lose my value. Then there is the whole matter of keeping up with the Joneses, which is especially important in affluent areas. This matter also touches the heart of family life, where children may not simply be loved and accepted for who they are, but are compared with one another and with the neighbors' children. "Act your age!" "Why can't you be good like your sister?" "What will the neighbors think?" These all-too-common household expressions can have very harmful effects.

At l'Arche, people quickly discover the human richness and true value of those who are at the bottom of a competitive society's caste system. This discovery destroys the meaning of such a caste system: no longer is it valid to give more respect to the doctor than to the cook, or to look down on the rejected, whether they are individuals with disabilities or prisoners or prostitutes. At l'Arche everyone tends to become identified with the disabled, with the rejected, and thus is freed from the fear of being rejected. One no longer needs to fear losing one's position after one has freely chosen to identify with those in the lowest position. This brings a kind of liberation to open oneself to the uniqueness of each and every person. Thus can begin that marvelous transformation from fearing what is different to loving what is different. Other persons and other ways of living are no longer a threat because they are different, but for that very reason are a source of enrichment that can release or generate great forces of creativity.

The men and women with developmental disabilities have little sense of competition. They prefer to share with others rather than compete with them. It is interesting to watch them at l'Arche on the playing field. They enjoy being together just throwing or kicking a ball around without choosing teams and turning it into a competition. Even when occasionally they do choose teams for a game of soccer, no one bothers to keep score. The joy comes from playing and not from trying to defeat someone. Doug McCarthy, a Jesuit from Canada, spent a summer at l'Arche in France. One afternoon he was helping people train for the Special Olympics. Claude was having a great time fooling around instead of trying to improve his running ability. Doug, losing patience, scolded him, saying, "Claude, if you don't smarten up, even Jean-Pierre is going to beat you." Jean-Pierre, being very spastic, could hardly walk, let alone run. Claude lit up with a great smile and said, "Wouldn't it be great if Jean-Pierre won!"

How important it is for a society in which the spirit of competition is destroying people's sense of self-worth and alienating them from each other, to make a place for people who are free of the spirit of competition, people who can help to call us into a life of sharing, where individuals are valued for themselves and their uniqueness.

We cannot simply abstract ourselves from this competitive society, but we can be sensitive to the criteria for what leads to greater wholeness within it. Seeking security in position and prestige or in conformity tends toward sterility. The tendency to categorize people or to show greater and lesser respect for some is also a sign of turning in on oneself and closing oneself off to life. The more we move to a greater sense of oneness with others, especially those whom our society tends to reject, the more we will discover wholeness and fullness of life. Living in greater fullness is just as much a gift as life itself. It cannot be achieved by our own power, but we can be more or less open to it and can look for it in the right or wrong places.

L'Arche began with the commitment of Jean Vanier, a man of position and much education, to share his life with Raphaël and Philippe, men of no position and little education. This was not so much something that Jean did with great courage but rather a gift he received with great openness. That commitment and that encounter between "rich" and "poor" was a gift for Jean and for Raphaël and Philippe, and it has generated extraordinary life and creativity. Jean was called out of the security of wealth and prestige into a life of great human insecurity. This has led him into the discovery of another, deeper kind of security: a security of faith in others and in the Other. His own faith leads him to speak of it in terms of an encounter with Jesus:

> Living with Raphaël and Philippe and many others who have become my brothers and sisters, I began to understand a little better the message of Jesus and his particular love for the poor in spirit and for the impoverished and weak ones of our society. I have learned much from them and feel deeply indebted to them. They have shown me what it is to live simply, to love tenderly, to speak in truth, to pardon, to receive openly, to be humble in weakness, to be confident in difficulties, and to accept handicaps and hardships with love. And, in a mysterious way, in their love they have revealed Jesus to me.[10]

Jean Vanier's response to a call coming through two individuals was the beginning of a life of community that has continued to open out toward the community of all people.

Community, like life, is a gift, and it begins with the commitment to open our lives to another. That is how we begin to build our own Ark to cross the sea that separates people. The more we make this commitment to those who are most rejected, the greater number of people that Ark will be able to welcome. The challenge to every community, whether it be a family or a congregation, is to respect the uniqueness of its members. Such a respect calls us to risk losing ourselves. A vital community must live in risk – open to the world and to the winds of change, not protecting itself with the false securities of possessions, popularity or power, but relying on the spirit of truth and love as its sole guarantee of survival and growth. It must realize that its weakest members are the most precious, and that its own fragility and weakness are a privilege. Strengths are what tend to separate individuals and groups, while weakness is a call to mutual support, sharing, and deeper communion. True community is not a ghetto protecting some people from others, but a place of encounter where people can meet in a true communion of minds and hearts. Every such community is a sign of hope and a proclamation that even in our divided world, there is enough room for joy.

Notes

1   Robert Speaight, *Vanier: Soldier, Diplomat and Governor General; A Biography* (Toronto: Collins, 1970), 256.

2   Eric Berne, *Games People Play: The Psychology of Human Relationships* (New York: Grove Press, 1964), 26.

3   Eric Berne, 25.

4   Eric Berne, 182.

5   Eric Berne, 180.

6   Eric Berne, 180.

7   Eric Berne, 181.

8   In 2004, as l'Arche celebrated its 40th anniversary, the International Federation consisted of 124 communities in 30 countries on five continents. Its developing history is presented in Jean Vanier's *An Ark for the Poor* (Ottawa: Novalis, 1995).

9   Henri Nouwen, *Creative Ministry* (Garden City, NY: Doubleday, 1971), 91.

10   Jean Vanier, *Eruption to Hope* (Toronto: Griffin House, 1971), preface.